THE COMPLETE BOOK OF
DECORATIVE
Knots

Lanyard knots
Button knots
Globe knots
Turk's heads
Mats
Hitching
Chains
Plaits

Geoffrey Budworth

The Lyons Press

contents

the knots

The Complete Book of Decorative Knots

First published in 1998 by Hamlyn
an imprint of Reed Consumer Books Limited
Michelin House, 81 Fulham Road, London SW3 6RB

Copyright © Reed Consumer Books Limited 1998

A CIP record for this book is available on file.

ISBN 1-55821-791-6

Publishing Director Laura Bamford

Executive Editor Mike Evans
Senior Editor Nina Sharman
Editor Caroline Bingham

Art Director Keith Martin
Executive Art Editor Mark Stevens
Illustration Line and Line

Production Bonnie Ashby

The publishers have made every effort to ensure that all
instructions given in this book are accurate and safe, but they
cannot accept liability for any resulting injury, damage or loss to
either person or property whether direct or consequential and
howsoever arising. The author and publishers will be grateful for
any information which will assist them in keeping future editions
up to date.

Typeset in Adobe Myriad, Monotype Walbaum and
Monotype Grotesque

Produced by Toppan Printing Co Ltd
Printed in China

DIRECTORY OF KNOTS

<6>

<7>

ACKNOWLEDGMENTS

Because knot tying is often a solitary pursuit I tend to say I am self-taught but that is not strictly true. Over more than 45 years I have absorbed much of what is in the hundreds of knot books I now own and so must gratefully acknowledge their writers and illustrators. In the 1960s and 70s I had a friend and knot-tying mentor, the late James Nicoll, who taught me a lot. Then, following the establishment in 1982 of the International Guild of Knot Tyers (IGKT), I was shown all kinds of original knot-working by my accomplished IGKT colleagues.

I especially acknowledge the following Guild members, in the U.K. and elsewhere, whose expertise has contributed directly or indirectly to the contents of this book: George Aldridge, Harry Asher, Percy Blandford, Dan Callahan (Alaska, USA), Jesse Coleman (Alabama, USA),

<8>

John Constable, Europa Chang Dawson, Ron Edwards, Brian Field, Gladys Findley, Eric Franklin, Stuart Grainger, Pieter van de Griend (The Netherlands), John Halifax, Tom Hall (Texas, USA), Frank Harris, Floris Hin (The Netherlands), Amund Karner (UK - Scotland), Kobierczynski Jurgen (Belgium), Jane Kennedy, Allan McDowall, Desmond Mandeville, Frans Masurel (The Netherlands), Des and Liz Pawson, Harold Scott, Theo Slijkerman (The Netherlands), Tom Solly, Charlie Smith, John Smith, Charles H.S. Thomason (Cairns, Australia), Brion Toss, and Jeff Wyatt.

Note: From this point on, individuals who are members of the IGKT will have those initials as a superscript after their names, for example, J. Smith[IGKT].

<9>

INTRODUCTION

Knots are more numerous than the stars;
and equally mysterious and beautiful.
Dr. John Turner[IGKT], Hamilton, New Zealand, 1988

It is possible to create elaborate ornamental knots without ever having learnt a simple practical one. In other words, you may tie a Turk's head but not have a clue about the timber hitch. You do not even have to like boats; a lot of land-based craftworkers and handicraft hobbyists make fancy knots, while other individuals choose to pursue this pleasurable craft for its own sake, finding knots as absorbing as solving a crossword puzzle or reading a good book. More than one avid knot tier has taken a length of cord aboard a commercial airliner, during a long-haul flight, and not only passed what might otherwise have been a tense or tedious trip enjoyably, but benefited from the personal attention of an interested cabin crew. And when Mariann Palmborg[IGKT], a Norwegian now living on the beautiful Caribbean island of Bequia, drives her jeep to the market, it is not merely to buy fruit, vegetables and a cool drink. She goes there to display and sell, beside the beautiful white sand beach, her decorative ropework products.

You can tackle one kind of decorative knotting – say button knots (see pp.60–79) – without knowing how to make a plait (see pp.128–154) or a mat (see pp.110–19). Just turn to any eye-catching page that takes your fancy, for there is no lengthy apprenticeship to be served here. Of course, it may be sensible to try a simpler knot before going on to tackle a more complex one in the same family – but even that is not a strict rule.

All knots have practical applications. As it happens, many of the more complicated ones also create appealing shapes and interwoven textures, but they too all evolved to serve some useful purpose or other. I started tying knots as an 11-year-old Sea Scout growing up on the south coast of England, where I was taught basic knots and splices; but it was not until I saw a specimen of decorative knotwork for the first time – a bellrope (combining plaits, lanyard and globe knots) – that I was truly smitten and knotting became for me a magnificent obsession that has lasted for almost 50 years. Now you too are about to be exposed to this infectious pastime. Always remember:

Knotting ventured,
knotting gained.

<10>

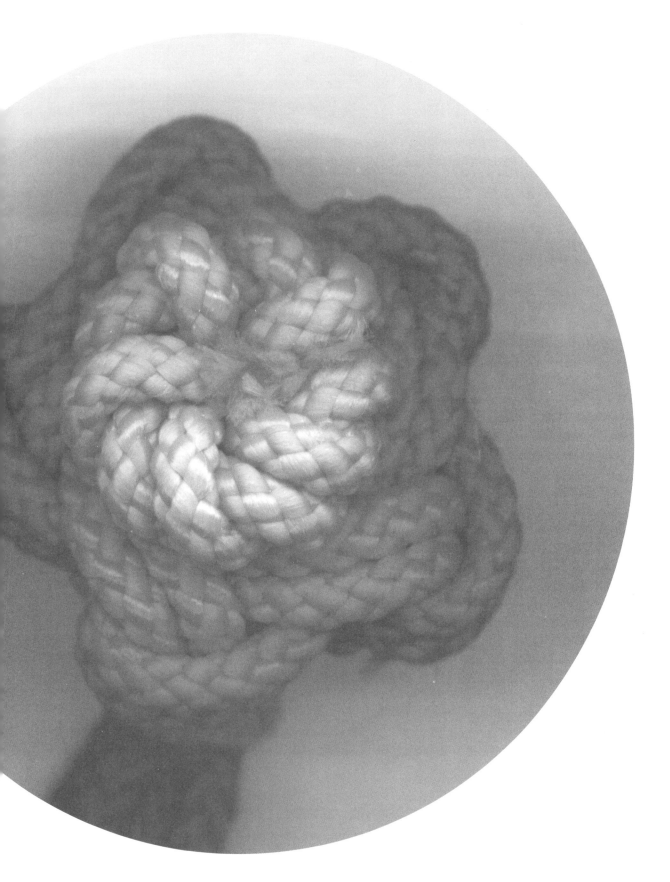

<11>

terms, tips and techniques

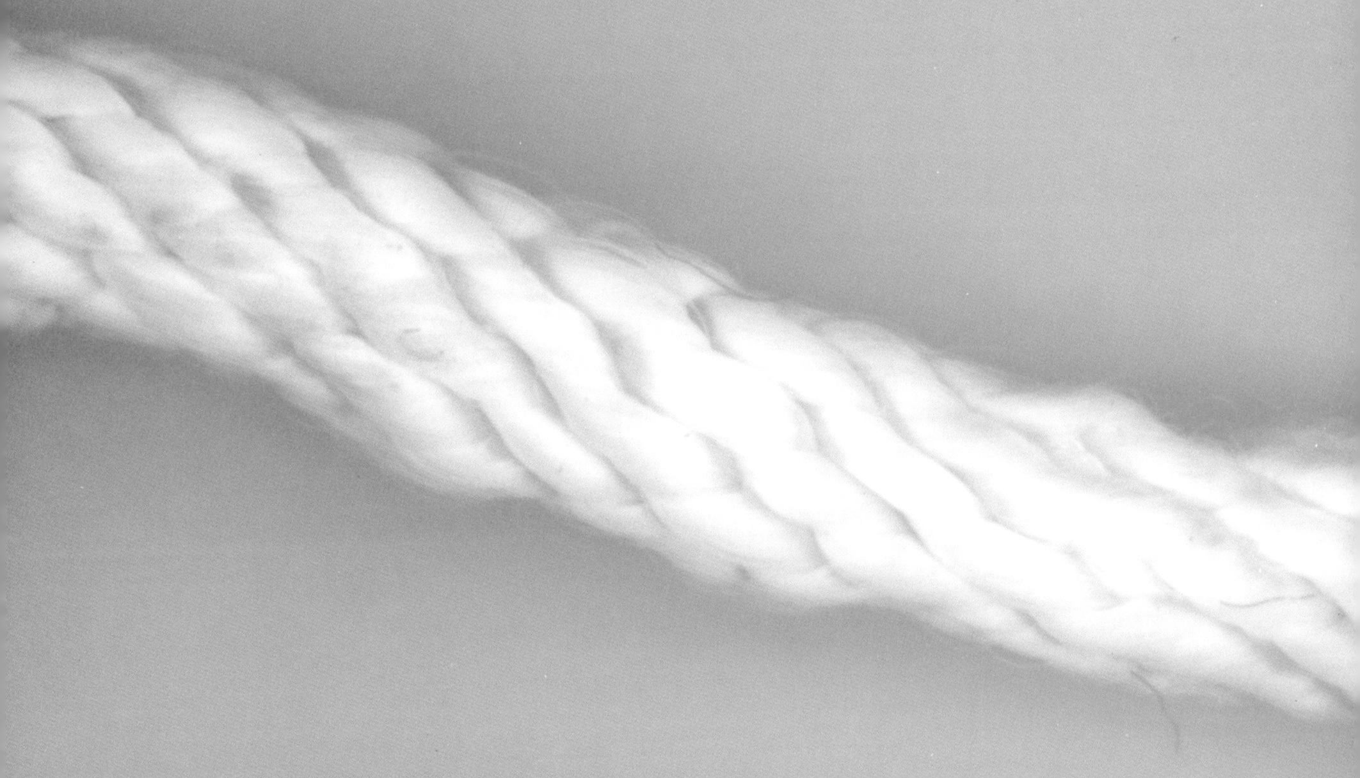

TERMS, TIPS AND TECHNIQUES

MATERIALS

Anything that may be twisted, tucked and interwoven, and plaited or braided, from torn lengths of fabric, silk threads and woollen yarns to rawhide thongs, twines, string, cord and rope, can be turned into some kind of knotwork. To learn more about the construction of rope and smaller cordage, see *The Hamlyn Book of Knots*; but for the knots contained in this volume it is enough to know that round flexible stuff (as it is informally called) with diameters not smaller than 3mm ($\frac{1}{8}$in) and probably not thicker than 10mm ($\frac{3}{8}$in) will do most things. Experiment to find out what best suits your fingers, eyesight and bank balance. You can purchase rope, cord and string by the metre from hardware shops or DIY superstores but – be warned – it is fairly expensive bought this way. Buying it by the cop (reel) should bring a discount of about 10%. Better still, locate and buy from the wholesaler who supplies the retailer. There are cheaper sources still:

for example, a camping shop is often less costly than a yacht chandlery or boat show, while a charity shop, car boot fair or boat jumble sale can yield treasures. Rummage in any bin of cut-price oddments before considering the stock on display, and get anything that attracts you there and then. You will find a use for it eventually.

Here is another money-saving tip. Many modern ropes and cords consist of a thin, braided outer sheath packed with a core of parallel yarns or filaments. Remove that core and the sheath becomes a flattened tape for such handiwork as coach-whipping or globe knots to cover hard spherical cores, which look better with a flat woven texture. The leftover core can be used (at no extra cost) for something else. To separate sheath from core, attach the filler strands to a firm anchorage, such as a doorknob (fig. 1), and then strip the sheath away, stripping up to 1m ($3\frac{1}{2}$ft) at a time with rhythmic swinging pulls from both hands.

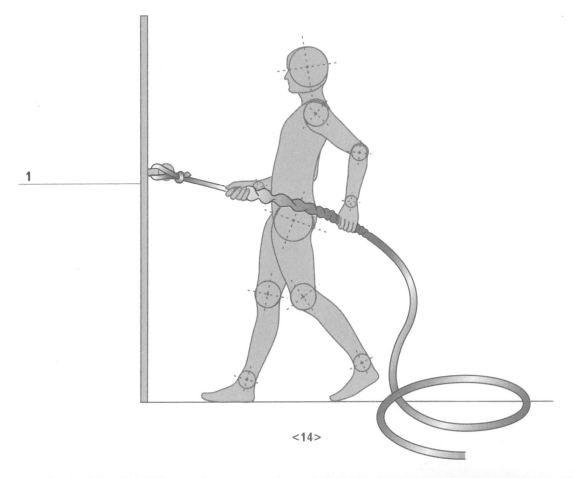

1

<14>

HEAT-SEALED ENDS

Synthetic (man-made) cordage can be cut and the ends sealed at the same time by heating a knife blade until it is cherry red and then severing the line in two wherever required. I use an old pocket knife and the noisy blue flame from my DIY blow-torch. The cooler yellow flame of a match will do, but it is neither as quick nor as neat. Various materials react differently: some melt cleanly, while others discolour; a few catch fire and burn with a small flame that is easily blown out. You soon learn how much heat to apply. With practice, ends may be sealed flat, rounded off, or squeezed to a point (with a wetted finger and thumb). Take care, however, as a melting gob of nylon, polyester, or whatever, will stick to skin and burn.

WORKING ENDS AND STANDING ENDS

The term 'working end' means the tip of a string, cord or rope which is tucked and tied, while the other (inactive) end is the 'standing end'.

SEIZING ENDS OR GATHERING STRANDS

Work with heat-sealed ends if you can, but they may have to be cut off altogether if they tend to snag the work. So, to prevent ends from fraying, or to gather several strands together temporarily, use a short length of thin cord or twine tied in a strangle knot (figs. 1–3), with or without a draw-loop for quick-release.

Strangle knot

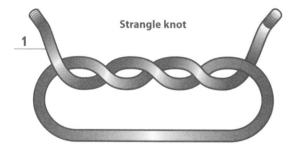

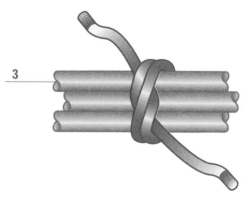

<15>

If you prefer it, a constrictor knot is just as effective. Wrap and tuck the working end as shown (figs. 4–6) and cut both ends off as short as you like. Sometimes it is possible to tie this knot slickly and quickly 'in the bight' (i.e. without using an end, see figs. 7–9). For tougher jobs, employ a double constrictor knot (fig.10) or simply tie two constrictors, one alongside the other. Two one-handed ways to assemble these knots are illustrated (figs. 11–14); or you can incorporate a draw-loop (figs. 15–16).

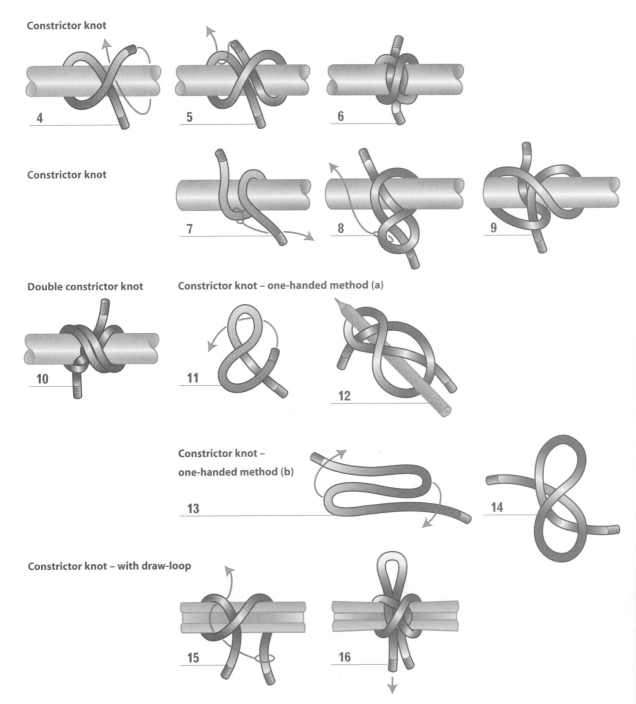

Constrictor knot

4

5

6

Constrictor knot

7

8

9

Double constrictor knot

10

Constrictor knot – one-handed method (a)

11

12

Constrictor knot – one-handed method (b)

13

14

Constrictor knot – with draw-loop

15

16

<16>

For extra security, when your seizing must be right on the end of whatever is being bound, consider the heavy-duty boa knot (figs. 17–20), which combines the characteristics of both strangle and constrictor knots. For the origins of the strangle, constrictor and boa knots, which are akin to medieval bag, sack or miller's knots, read *The Hamlyn Book of Knots*. Meanwhile, a poem of mine (which first appeared in the March 1997 issue of *Knotting Matters* (KM), the quarterly magazine of the IGKT, summarizes this gripping trio thus:

> The Bag, Sack and Miller's Knots
> Are rudimentary bindings;
> But often ropework jobs need lots
> Of more elaborate windings.
>
> The aptly named Constrictor
> Will cling and grip like glue, Sir!
> While the Strangle Knot's a stricture
> Some deem neater – and no looser.
>
> But the Boa's the toughest
> (superb hybrid, new begot*);
> Stronger, bulkier than the rest,
> Belt-and-braces in one knot.

> *Devised in 1996 by the eminent weaver and craft writer Peter Collingwood.

Boa knot in the bight

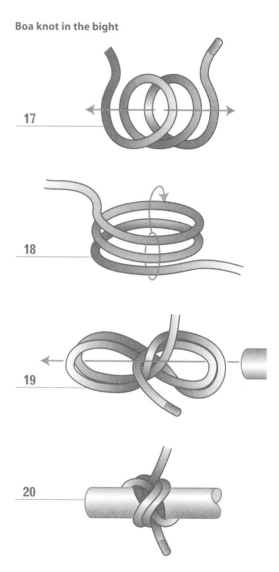

17

18

19

20

Boa knot from a working end

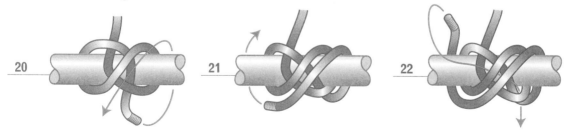

20

21

22

<17>

TOOLS

To start with, fingers will suffice. Soon, however, a few bits and pieces will prove helpful: a 1m (3½ft) rule to measure out lengths of cord; scissors and a sharp craft knife to cut and trim strands; some tracing paper and sheets of graph (or other squared) paper, with a B or 2B pencil and an eraser, to draw or copy and enlarge knot patterns; a cork or thick polystyrene tile of some sort (fig. 1), together with a lot of macrame T-pins (available from craft shops) to stake out your knots over their drawings.

Some knotwork is completed more easily, or made neater, with tools; while tucking, tightening and burying ends is sometimes impossible without them. Many of the implements listed and described below were actually made for riggers and sailmakers, but every one of them can help to tie knots:

Fids (fig. 2) are traditional splicing tools. These tapered wooden spikes are used for prising rope strands apart prior to tucking other strands between them. Hand-held ones made of lignum vitae or other hardwoods come in various sizes, from about 10cm (4in) long up to 30cm (1ft) or more. Many second-hand fids are now antique items, at collectors' prices, but new ones can be bought more reasonably.

Marlinespikes (fig. 3) are versatile metal implements, with either pointed or wedge-shaped tips, intended for splicing rope or wire. Sizes vary from as short as 10cm (4in) to heavyweight versions upwards of 30cm (1ft) in length, and they usually have an eye to which a lanyard may be attached. Use the pointed end for poking and the thick end for pounding knots into the desired shape.

Prickers (fig. 4) are smaller metal spikes, between 10–25cm (4–10in) long, with wooden handles.

Swedish fids (fig. 5) have been around since at least the 1960s, when the early ones were stamped 'Made in Sweden' (hence the name). They resemble cheese or apple corers. Their stainless steel concave cross-section retains a space through which strands can be inserted, in contrast to the traditional solid wood fid which has to be withdrawn before any tucking can be done. As the tool is removed, the strand is pulled through with it. Tool lengths start at about 15cm (6in) and go up to a heavy-duty 38cm (15in) version.

<18>

6

Gripfids (fig. 6) resemble small Swedish fids but are made from hand-forged brass, polished and lacquered, each with a Turk's head handle. The characteristic that gives a gripfid its name, however, is the 1–2cm ($\frac{1}{2}$–1in) of the edges near the point which are burred over so that the tool nips and holds the cord, pulling it through as the implement is withdrawn. They are an invention from the brain and workshop of knot craftsman and writer Stuart Grainger[IGKT], a Guild past-President; and many of us would not be without a couple, since the standard size fits cordage up to about 7mm ($\frac{1}{4}$in) diameter and a larger version copes with up to 12mm ($\frac{1}{2}$in) diameter strands.

7

Wire loops of various sizes (fig. 7) are perhaps the single most useful tool for decorative knot tying but they often have to be home-made, from stiff and springy 2.5mm ($\frac{1}{8}$in) diameter (or thinner) wire, inserted into a handle and secured so that it will not pull out again. Periodically an IGKT member will have a batch for sale. As the loops are flat, they go where a fatter fid will not. Their big snag is that the strands, yarns or threads pulled through are doubled (and consequently twice as thick), which can be a struggle and may disfigure the completed job. One way around this is, if possible, to pull only a few yarns through at a time.

8
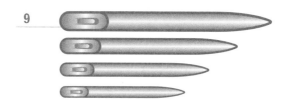

Tubular fids (fig. 8) are plastic or aluminium tubes, pointed at one end and open at the other. They are produced and sold by rope manufacturers for splicing their own sheath-&-core products, and for that reason there are several sizes available for different diameters of rope.

Pushers (not illustrated) are long, knitting needle-like implements used to extend the range of tubular fids. There is a small size for 6–14mm ($\frac{1}{4}$–$\frac{1}{2}$in) diameter strands and a larger version for (16–24mm ($\frac{5}{8}$–1in) diameters.

9

Nesting tubular fids (fig. 9) make a splendid present for anyone who does a lot of difficult knotwork. Mine are in a Norwegian 'Selma' stainless steel set with a range of sizes for strands from 4–20mm ($\frac{1}{8}$–$\frac{3}{4}$in) diameter.

10

Splicing needles (fig. 10) are metal and there are a variety of brand names. They may be supplied by ropemakers within packaged splicing kits. They come in small, medium and extra-long sizes and are used like wire loops.

<19>

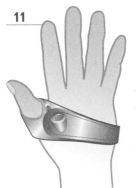

Sailmaker's palms (fig. 11) are leather or other tough hand-straps, each with a thumb hole (biased for left- or right-handed users), to which is affixed a dimpled metal socket, so that the heel of the hand can push large needles through rope or canvas.

Round-billed pliers (fig. 12) are used to tighten knots. They can be obtained in a small size (sometimes referred to as 'jeweller's pliers') about 1 cm (4½in) overall length, and in more robust sizes from about 15cm (6in) upwards.

Netting needles (fig. 13), available in plastic, wood or even metal (not ideal), are a traditional way to store and work tangle-free with substantial hanks of cord, string or the finest twines. Sizes range from a slim and short 15cm (6in) to jumbo-sized ones 30cm (1ft) or more in length, and occasionally you may find one nicely narrowed into a waist for a comfortable grip. Avoid roughly made ones in preference to those that are smoothly rounded and finished. Your supplier will show you how to load them with line.

Needles (not illustrated). Collect a variety of the larger kinds (rug-making, sacking, sailmaking), particularly when they have big eyes and bluntish points. I have recently been given two robust ones made by Dan Callahan[IGKT] of Anchorage, Alaska. They are tubular, approximately 2mm (⅛in) and 4mm (¼in) in diameter, but the special feature is that each one has at its blunt end an internal screw thread. The idea – and it works well – is to heat and soften the end of nylon or other synthetic line so that it can be screwed into the needle; then, once tucking or threading has been successfully done, it can be unscrewed, detached, and (if necessary) re-attached to the same or another working end.

Pin vices (fig. 14) are hand-held engineering chucks that grip any needle or other pointed spike of slender diameter, transforming it into a pricker. I use a couple of sizes, both less than 10cm (4in) long.

From the list above it is clear that knot tyers adopt and adapt tools from other trades and callings, whenever they may prove handy with rope and cordage. Rooting through my own tool-box I find that some of the diverse oddities I have accumulated over half a century include a pair of end-cutting pliers intended for typewriter mechanics, an awl for repairing cane chair seats, a lacing tool for old-fashioned leather footballs, a bodkin from a stationer's shop (to attach pink ribbon to legal papers), and some warping posts used by weavers to measure and cut long strands.

<20>

HOW TO DRAW KNOT PATTERNS

To devise an original flat knot layout (such as fig. 1), or to copy and enlarge one from a book like this, it helps to use graph or other squared paper. First try to spot how crossing points often occur in a regular pattern, which can be reproduced by means of pencilled Xs on the paper (fig. 2) and then joined up. This eliminates freehand guesswork. Note, too, how the bight (see **Glossary**) at the top of this particular pattern has been broken into a standing end and working end; endless knot designs may look artistic, but in cordage they have to be tied, although the standing end and working end may be located anywhere within the knot. This particular pattern is a traditional sailor's breast plate design, intended to be worn on the chest, hanging from a cord around the neck.

Starting at the lead (say 'leed') with the arrowhead (fig. 3), mark each crossing point alternately *over* or *under*. In recent years leading knot writers have begun to shorten long under-over tucking sequences to the letters U-O-U (as appropriate), and I shall do the same. Continue until the whole layout has been marked in this way. Then, for a pin-&-tuck working plan, simply draw the U-O-U sequence with a thick felt-tip pen (fig. 4). Otherwise, you might insert a double line (fig. 5) and again reproduce the U-O-U regular basket weave sequence (fig. 6).

Knot drawings can be enlarged or reduced: by hand and eye; by scaling them up or down with squared paper; or you may possess a pantograph (even a toy one will do). But, these days, take difficult or tedious drawings to the nearest photocopier with an enlarging and reducing function. It is also possible to photocopy real knots, certainly for working purposes, and even occasionally for publication. Simply place the knotwork on the machine and put the cover down. Try it and see for yourself.

<21>

TUCKING CORDS OR STRANDS

When a single strand knot is to be doubled (followed around a second time), first fold the cord in half to locate the centre ('middle' it) and use only one half to tie the knot. This saves pulling through a lot of surplus line. Then, once the knot is completed, the other half can be used for the doubling process.

Never tuck a long working end if, instead, you can pick up a bight close to the work in hand and tuck that first (fig. 1). Slide any needle or wire loop involved to within 15cm (6in) of the tucking point. Then, once the tuck is done and the needle or loop (if any) has emerged, pull all the surplus line through until the end is reached. This way, problems of twisting and kinking will resolve themselves as the loose end is free to shed any such torsion.

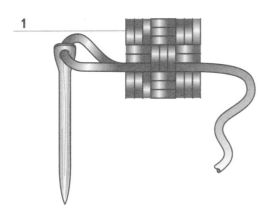

1

Clifford Ashley recommended wearing a sleeveless pullover and sitting on a backless stool to tie knots with lengthy strands. It remains good advice. If ends are not to become snarled on furniture, snared by hooks and knobs and catches and handles, ensure you are in a snag-free zone.

ADDING, OR REDUCING, STRANDS

Estimate the length of working strands needed and then add a bit for luck before you cut them, so that, ideally, none turns out to be too short. It is not possible to say just how much cord every knot requires; but, as it will be loosely tied and then tightened, it always takes more than the finished

item. Some simple plaits or braids use only one-third as much again as the completed length of work; but a multi-strand chain plait of repeated crown knots might absorb six or more times the finished length. In the case of knots pinned loosely onto a board over an expanded drawing, five to ten times the final length may be necessary – although much of that will be retrieved in tightening and may then be cut off for re-use on another project.

It is just about impossible to add a fresh strand to an exhausted one, without it showing, by merely knotting one to the other. If, however, the addition of a knot at intervals within the work is not an eyesore, then a few can be recommended:

Fisherman's knot (figs. 2–6). This is also a neat way (especially doubled (figs. 7–9) or trebled: figs. 10–12) to unite the two cords of a neck lanyard.

Fisherman's knot

2

3

4

5

front view

6

rear view

<22>

Fisherman's knot doubled

7

8

9

Fisherman's knot trebled

10

11

12

Overhand bend (figs. 13–14). Climbers and cavers will know this knot, tied in flat or tubular tap (webbing), as the tape knot.

13

14

One-way, back-tucked sheet bend (figs.15–18). The two working ends should lay alongside the standing part of the exhausted strand, with the single standing part being the newly attached cord.

15

16

17

18

<23>

Tumbling thief knot (figs. 1–5). This little known knot, devised by the late Desmond Mandeville[IGKT], is tricky to assemble and draw up snug; but he discovered – after testing many bends (i.e. joining knots) by pulling them through holes of decreasing diameter – that this was the thinnest knot he knew.

Thicker cords may be laid parallel to one another, overlapping a few centimetres (two or three inches), and both worked until the old strand is left behind and the fresh one goes on alone. Later it will be necessary to conceal both of those ends by burying them beneath the work. If the additional bulk this

doubling up causes is unacceptable, then some sort of ad hoc thinning and splicing may be resorted to. By removing a section of the heart strands from larger diameter sheath-&-core cordage, it is often possible to insert one into the other with a wire loop or tubular fid; twines, embroidery threads, knitting or rug wools, might be twisted together with scarcely any noticeable thickening; or, with care, the ends of strands may be cut square or sliced diagonally and super-glued together.

Taper multi-strand work by leaving out a strand here and there as you progress. This is easier than adding them, and later having to bury more than you started with. So always consider starting at the thick end of a piece of work (rather than the other way round).

Tumbling thief knot

19

21
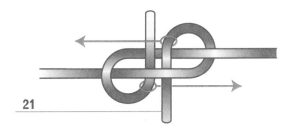

20
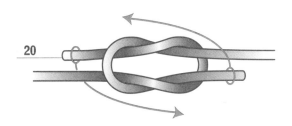

22

23

<24>

TIGHTENING KNOTS

Fancy knots ought generally to appear as if sculpted from a solid medium, so they must be pulled firm and tight. It is easiest to tie a knot loosely, so that all of the tucks can be readily made, but that entails the subsequent removal of a lot of slack. Alternatively, it is possible to tie a knot fairly tight from the outset, with each succeeding tuck tightening it still more; then, when the last tuck is done, there is nothing more to do. Some knot tyers work that way, but the final few tucks can be a real struggle to achieve, and too much rough handling spoils the finished appearance of knots. (Anyway, all that sweaty wrestling risks a pricked or impaled finger, with blood-stains on the end product!) Compromise and practise something between the two, tucking and tying with as little slack as possible, while keeping the tucks fairly easy to do. Then finish off with just one (maybe two) rounds of tightening.

Working with a single strand, start at one end and progress along the cord, carefully levering up any slack with fingers and a spike as you go (fig. 1). You may prefer to use round-billed pliers with a rolling action (fig. 2). Either way, do not overdo it. Excessive and uneven tension may disfigure your cleverly made knot and ruin it. Tightening a knot is every bit as critical as tying it in the first place. In a single strand knot, a sizeable slack bight will develop, so never put such a half-done knot down in that state – to answer the phone or doorbell – unless you are sure which way is forward. When you pick it up again, there is a 50/50 chance that you may mistakenly back-track, undoing and messing up your earlier work. It happens. When you have tightened and tensioned a few of the more elaborate single-strand knots, you will welcome the easier multi-strand ones.

While they look more complex, each individual strand of a multi-strand knot is only a fraction as complicated. Starting near to the standing ends, pull a little slack from one knot part, and then repeat the process (at the same or an

equivalent spot) with each and every cord or strand in turn, until you have a small bight for every one. Follow around methodically, completing one cycle before going on to do the same thing at the next point, until you finally emerge at the working ends. Do not yield to the temptation of progressing further with one strand than the others, or – as with single strand knots – you may distort the knot irremediably. If it happens, there is often no solution except to untie it completely and begin again.

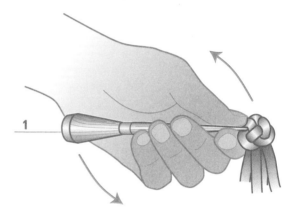

1

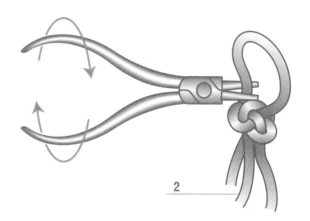

2

<25>

BURYING STRANDS

Much of the ornamental ropework seen in yacht clubs and Scout meeting rooms, pubs and other public places, ends in tassels or fringes. These may be intentional embellishments, but more often – I suspect – the tyer did not bother to bury the ends. Knotwork is not finished until the ends have been hidden away, leaving no clue in many instances to how it was begun and where it ended. "My knots aren't tied", my old knotting mentor, James Nicoll, would grin, "they just happen".

To bury ends, use needles, wire loops or tubular fids (depending upon the size and scale of the handiwork) to insert or pull the short, cut ends beneath the surface of your knotwork. Leave sufficient slack to do so; or bury them before pulling everything tight. Then cut the strands off flush against the surface of the completed work and push what remains out of sight with the point of a fid, pricker or needle. If you pull hard on some strands, while cutting them, the severed end will shrink out of sight like a wounded worm. There is no single way to bury every end. The process can demand a lot of ingenuity but it should not be avoided. If a display piece has a back or underside (that will not be seen), I contrive it so that all the loose ends emerge there, and I seal them all with a hot knife blade; but, as they harden and may discolour, that can only be done where it will not show.

GLUES AND HARDENERS

Centuries ago, ropemakers weather-proofed ships' rigging by impregnating it with hot tar. Riggers and sailors often wrapped and stitched individual knot strands into canvas and either tarred or painted them. There is no need for that messiness with modern cordage. Some knot tyers, however, do treat their finished knotwork with proprietory preparations; for example, yacht varnish will waterproof outdoor knotwork, although it tends to darken the original colour.

Brian Field[IGKT] and Jeff Wyatt[IGKT] – two admirable knot craftsmen – stiffen, toughen and dirt-proof many of their knotty artifacts with a water-soluble PVA (polyvinyl acetate) craft glue. One that dries white does for white cordage, but they prefer an all-purpose clear variety. The colour of some cords may be slightly altered by this treatment, but not enough to discourage its use, and the degree of stiffening that results depends upon the type of cord. Dilute the hardener with water to no more than a 50/50 solution (60% glue to 40% water is best) in a suitable container to dip and soak the knotwork. Try cutting a large lemonade bottle in half. Once you have dipped the cord, wait for any air bubbles to stop, which may take only a few seconds, before lifting it out and blowing briefly on any flooded textural surface features to remove surplus solution before it goes too gooey. Then hang it above the container to drip dry for up to an hour. This allows as much mixture as possible (often as much as 80%) to drain back into the reservoir for re-use. Hairy cords may, at this stage, bristle like alarmed hedgehogs. Do not worry and do not try to remedy their appearance right now. Never dip cord twice – that would ruin the appearance – and, in the case of a necklet, do not dip the neck thong itself, which must be kept flexible. Complete the drying process by leaving for 24 hours over a radiator or in an airing cupboard. Then, if the work is still marred by spiky filaments, briefly expose them to the flame of a cigarette lighter (not too close), rotating the work to minimise the heat on any one part. The offending bits will shrivel to insignificance.

<26>

MULTIPLE OVERHAND KNOTS

Learn these simple ornamental knots tied in a single strand to separate beads threaded on a string, or as neat stopper knots to prevent cords from fraying or pulling out of holes. You may have spotted them as embellishments in the ropes tied around the waists of nuns and monks. Getting to grips with these knots now is likely to help when it comes to tightening Matthew Walker knots (see pp. 55–9). First tie a simple overhand or thumb knot (fig.1), with a draw-loop (fig. 2) for easy untying if you like. Tuck the working end a second time to create a double overhand knot (figs. 3–5). Begin to tighten the knot by pulling gently on both ends – feel how it wants to twist and wrap around itself. Allow it to do so, turning the left-hand end up and away from you, and the right-hand one down and toward you (assuming you are using the knot in the diagram; for its mirror image, reverse these instructions). Another tuck creates a triple overhand knot (figs. 6–8) which requires even more care in shaping the final form.

Double overhand knot

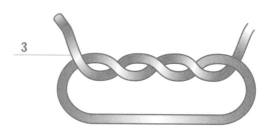

Simple overhand or thumb knot

Triple overhand knot

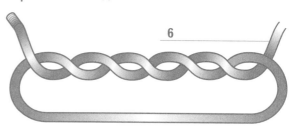

Simple overhand knot with draw-loop

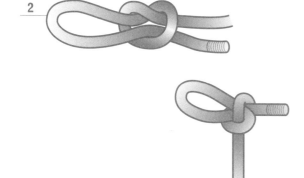

<27>

CROWN KNOTS

Crown knots do not stand alone but combine with other knots to form compound ones. Three-strand (fig. 1), four-strand (fig. 2), five-strand (fig. 3), or more, they all serve to return the working strands back upon themselves. Note how the first bight (see **Glossary**) in the sequence must be kept open until the final locking tuck can be made. With more than four strands, a space is inevitable in the heart of the knot, and so they are tied around another rope.

Crown knots will close up and cling better around foundations with wide diameters if each strand in turn goes over *two* and under *two* (or three) adjacent strands (figs. 4–8).

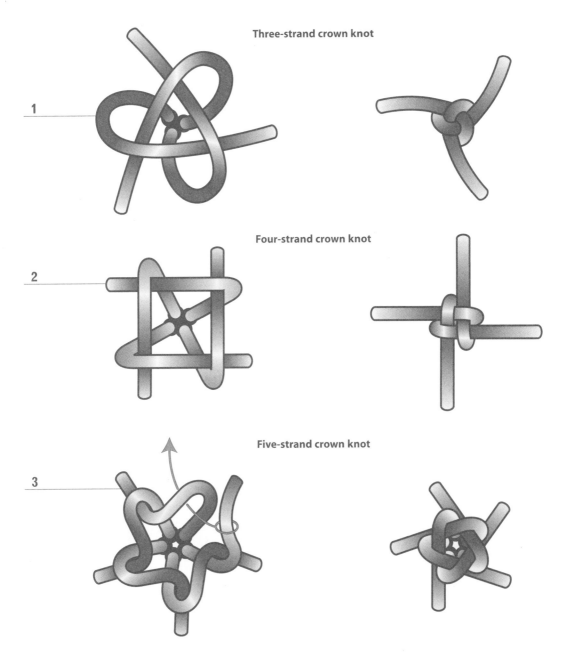

Three-strand crown knot

1

Four-strand crown knot

2

Five-strand crown knot

3

<28>

Complex crown

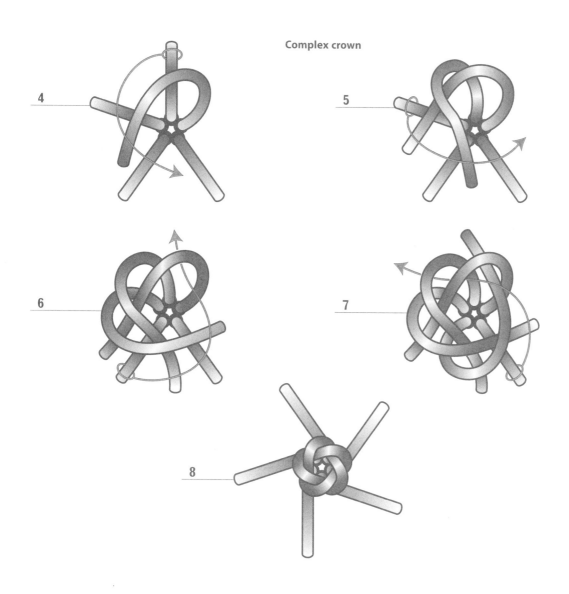

KEY TO THE SYMBOLS

 Lanyard knots

 Mats and hitching

 Clockwise crown or wall knot

 Button and globe knots

 Plaits and braids

 Anti-clockwise crown or wall knot

 Turk's heads

<29>

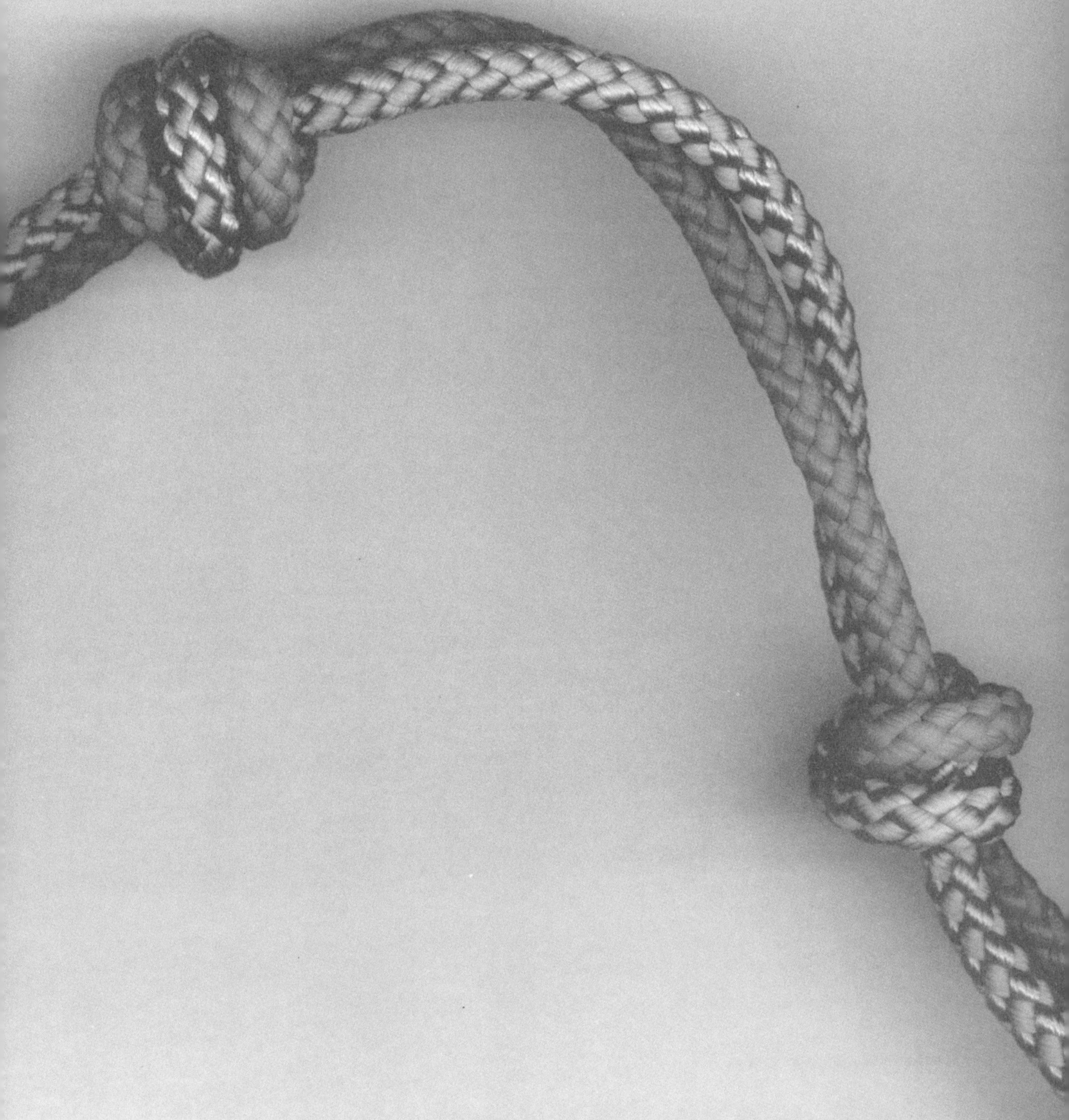

LANYARD KNOTS

A lanyard (earlier spelling: laniard or lanierd) is any short piece of line fastened to an object to secure it or to act as a handle. At sea it refers more particularly to lines that secure shrouds and stays (the standing rigging that braces masts).

Lanyard knots were originally used as stopper knots to retain a lanyard's end within its deadeye (static block) and prevent it fraying. These days they can be used to embellish a single strand or separate beads on a necklace. They can also seize together two or more parallel strands at the start of a plait or braid, as well as form simple and compound decorative knots. Lanyard knots can be applied to mark and mask a changeover in the pattern of braids or plaits and hitching used on long items of knotwork, such as bellropes, dog leashes, barrier ropes, light pulls, lanyards and necklaces. The characteristic of any lanyard knot is that the strands always enter at one end of the knot and leave at the other end.

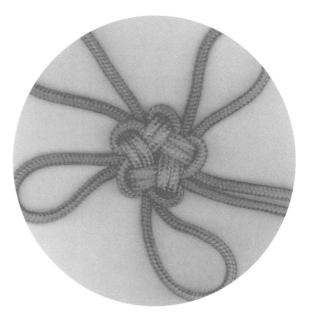

Five-part good luck knot

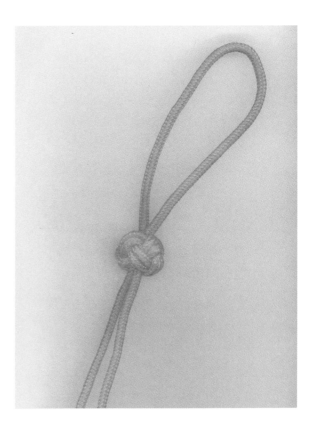

Knife lanyard doubled

<32>

LANYARD LOOPS

A lanyard usually ends in a loop to which may be
attached anything from a whistle to a knife, a key or
a good-luck charm. Make that loop at least as long as
the object to be attached (fig. 1), which must be
threaded onto it and then passed through to create
a ring hitch (fig. 2).

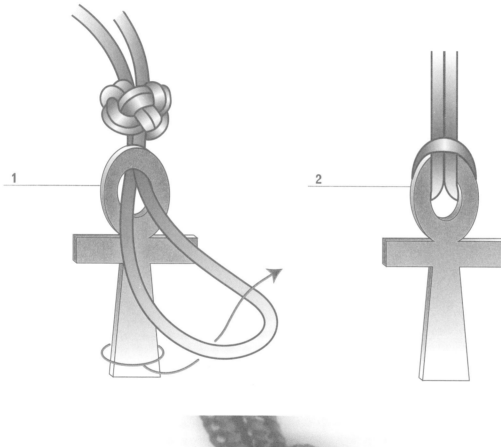

<33>

BLIMP KNOT

APPLICATIONS
This is a nicely symmetrical ornamentation for an otherwise uninteresting length of cord.

METHOD
Tie a figure eight knot (fig. 1) and then tuck each working end back through it to complete the job (fig. 2). Alternatively, tie an overhand knot (fig. 3) and tuck the working end as shown.

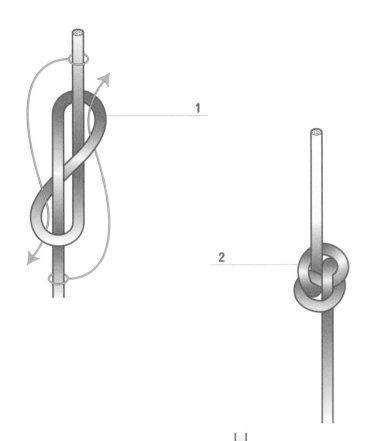

1

2

HISTORY
The pre-eminent knotting writer Clifford W. Ashley, whose monumental *The Ashley Book of Knots* is every avid knot tyer's bible, does not single this knot out either to state that it is original (so presumably it was already known when he published his book in 1944), or to name it. I call it the Blimp* because it resembles a Zeppelin bend (see *The Hamlyn Book of Knots*) but is smaller and softer.
*Blimp: a light, non-rigid aircraft such as a barrage balloon.

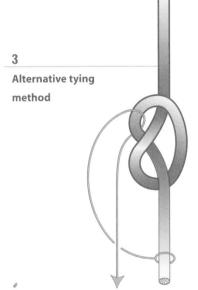

3

Alternative tying method

<34>

BRAID KNOT

APPLICATIONS

It shortens and adds attractive bulk to a light pull, waist-tie, friendship braid, or whatever. In thicker material it creates a superb makeshift handle for a travelling case. I use one plaited in 10mm (⅜in) diameter braided rope to raise the dagger plate of my sailing dinghy.

METHOD

Arrange the starting layout (fig. 1) and then make a three-strand plait (figs. 2–3). The working end will gradually tangle in a loose mirror-image of what you are producing with the working parts of the material. Pause whenever necessary to untangle it. When the bottom loop has only room left for one more tuck, make that tuck and the knot is complete.

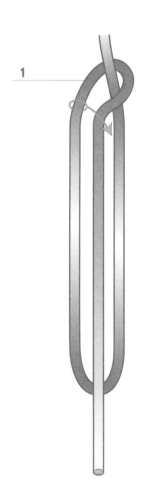

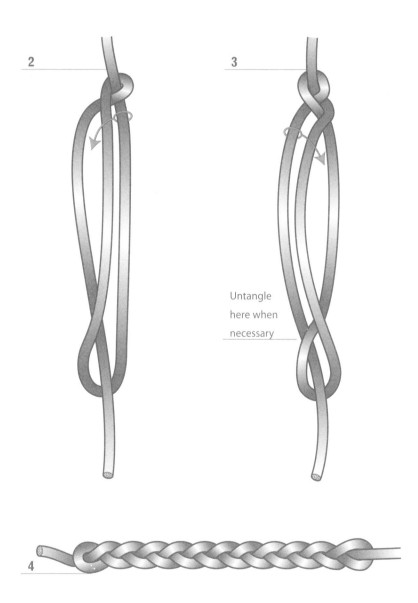

Untangle here when necessary

<35>

CHINESE CLOVERLEAF

APPLICATIONS

In soft thick cord this makes a striking ornamentation, and it also looks fine in more delicate silk braids.

METHOD

It is possible to tie this knot (figs. 1–2) directly in the hand, copying the step-by-step illustrations. Otherwise, hold it down on a flat surface. Nurse carefully into the final shape, removing slack patiently a bit at a time. Do not rush the process. Once the knot is pulled out of shape, it may be impossible to recover it. However, when all the daylight has been removed from the box-like heart (fig. 3), the finished shape will become inevitable. Leave the three leaf-like bights, if you prefer, or eliminate them altogether for a square and solid knot (figs. 4–5).

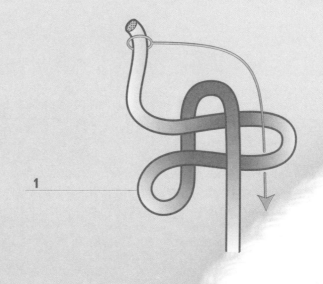

1

2

<36>

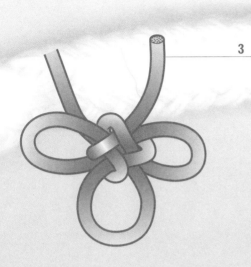

3

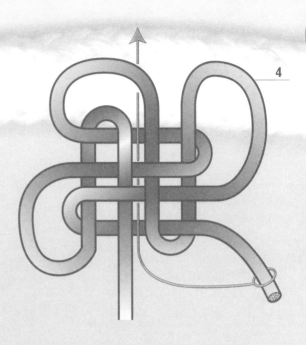

4

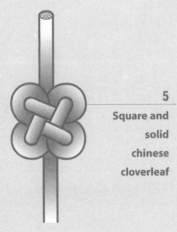

5

**Square and
solid
chinese
cloverleaf**

HISTORY

Evidence of Chinese
decorative knotting survives only
from the late Ching and early
Republican periods of the past century or
so; but there is circumstantial evidence that
it evolved over perhaps a thousand years.
Chinese arts and crafts differ markedly from
western ones and their knots are no
exception, but the folklore attached to the
cloverleaf is the same (good luck,
especially if a four-leaved one
can be found).

<37>

OBLONG KNOT

APPLICATIONS
Ornamental.

METHOD
This is an elaboration of the Chinese cloverleaf knot on
pages 36–7. Because there are more knot parts and
crossings (figs. 1–7), be even more careful and patient in
tightening this version.

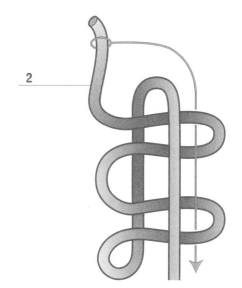

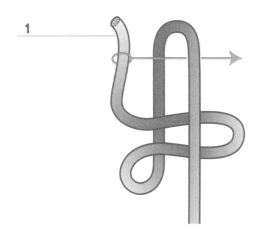

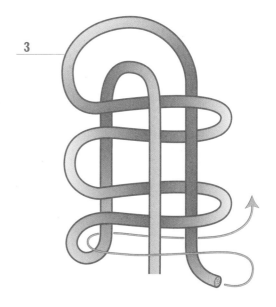

<38>

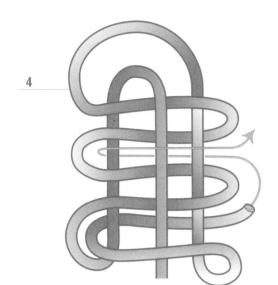

4

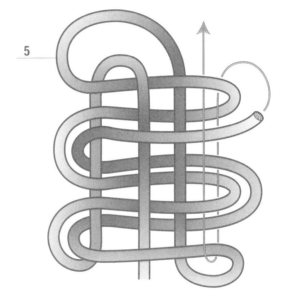

5

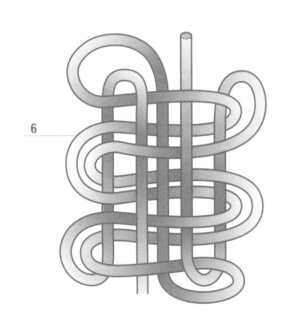

6

7

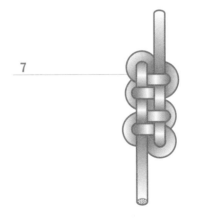

<39>

MYSTIC KNOT

APPLICATIONS
Ornamental.

METHOD
Pin this knot out over an expanded diagram on a cork or polystyrene mat. Arrange the first stage in the layout with one working end (fig. 1) and then switch to what was originally the standing end for the remainder of the tying process (figs. 2–3). As this seemingly two-dimensional shape is tightened, a top and a bottom layer separate to give unsuspected extra depth. Let it happen. The knot may be tightened altogether, or left with loops showing (fig. 4).

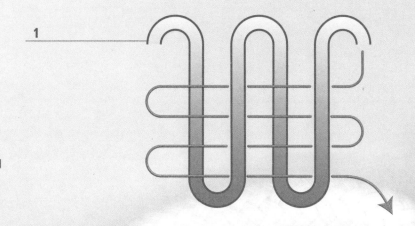

<40>

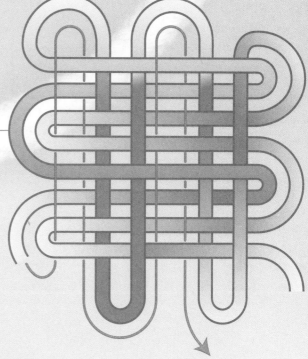

HISTORY

One of the basic precepts of Chinese Buddhism is the cyclical nature of all existence and this apparently endless knot pattern embodies that concept. Lydia Chen, in her superb manual *Chinese Knotting*, states that the mystic knot is one of the eight Buddhist treasures and she calls it by its alternative name, Pan Chang Knot.

3

4

PECTORAL KNOT

APPLICATIONS

This triangular knot may be displayed at chest level on any necklace or lanyard.

METHOD

It is possible to tie this knot directly in the hand, like the Chinese cloverleaf (see p. 36), but you have more chance of completing a pectoral knot at the first attempt if it is pinned out on an expanded diagram in the same way as the preceding mystic knot (figs. 1–4). The two upper corner loops (fig. 5) are then attached to a neck thong and any bead, ornament or mascot is tied to the two working ends with a two-strand lanyard knot.

<42>

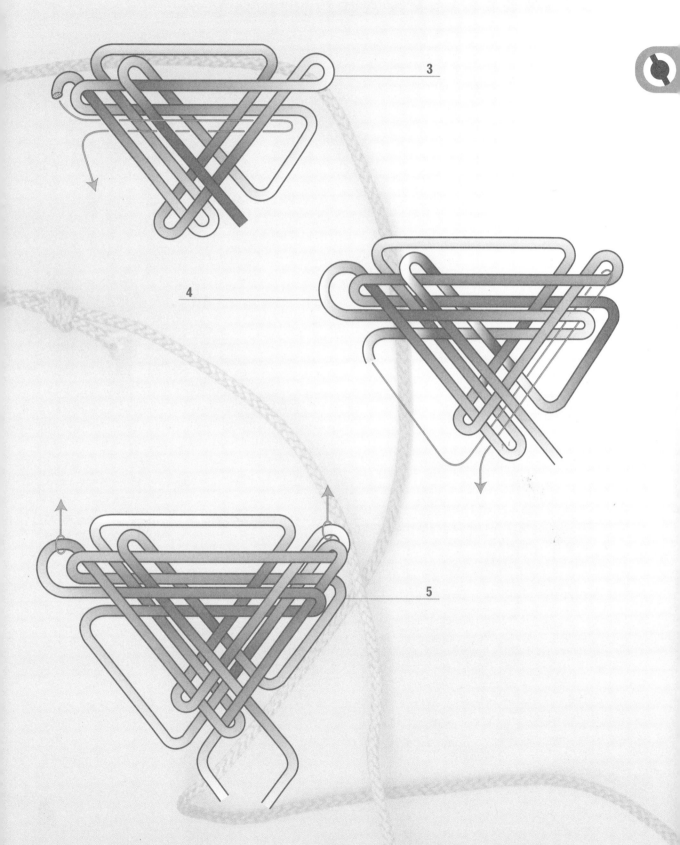

3

4

5

<43>

CHINESE LANYARD KNOT

APPLICATIONS

This symmetrical – but subtly so – bulky two-strand knot will decorate anything from a necklet to a tool lanyard, make earrings (in finer cord), or you might tie it just for the fun of doing so.

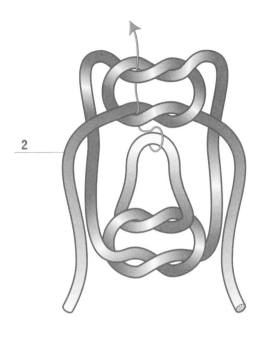

2

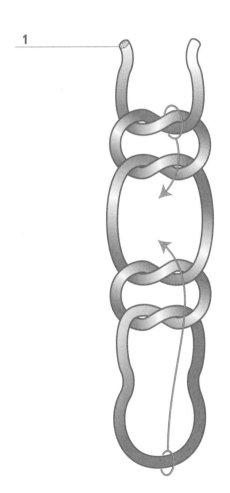

1

METHOD

Fold the cord in the middle and tie four identical half knots (fig. 1), keeping them separated as two matching pairs of granny knots.

Invert each pair (fig. 2) and pull the elongated loop up through the centre of the facing pair of half knots (which will make more sense if you have already tied a solomon or bannister bar, see p. 142). Similarly, pass both ends down through the middle of the remaining two half knots (fig. 3) exactly as illustrated; no other way will work. Tighten cautiously – a bit at a time. Deform this knot and it will never come right. There is no one right way, but I suggest that – to start with – you ensure the overlapping four-leaved heart is firm and snug (fig. 4); then pull the two side loops out to close top and bottom half knots (fig. 5). Now it becomes more tedious than difficult. Work the slack from each side loop through the knot until it either emerges at the loop or, preferably, via one or other of the two ends, to arrive at the completed knot (fig. 6).

<44>

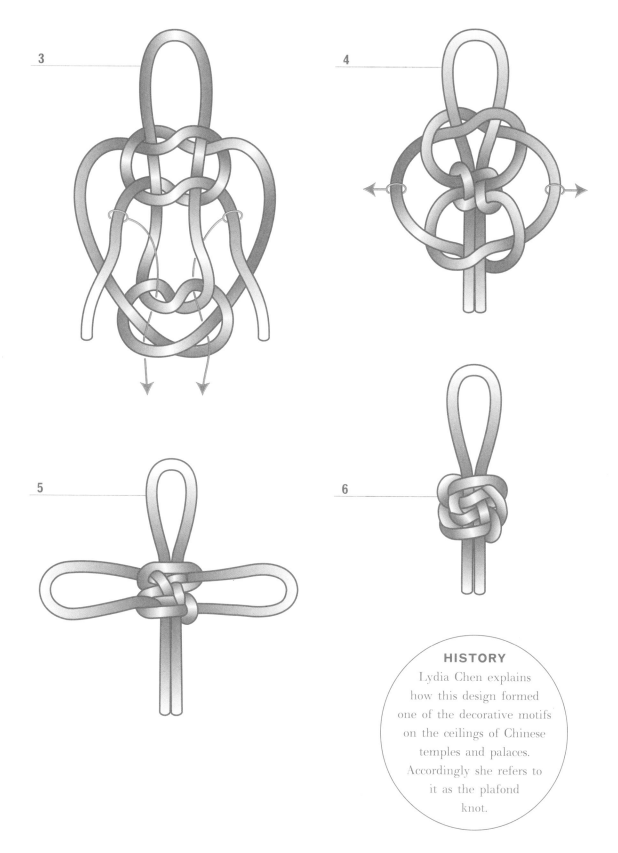

3

4

5

6

HISTORY
Lydia Chen explains
how this design formed
one of the decorative motifs
on the ceilings of Chinese
temples and palaces.
Accordingly she refers to
it as the plafond
knot.

<45>

GOOD LUCK KNOT

APPLICATIONS

Embellish a gift-wrapped parcel with this knot, hang it around your neck (or give one to a friend) or on your front door during any festive season, or use it as a complex of belt loops for keys or tools.

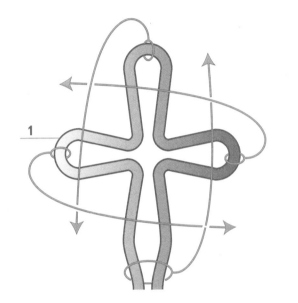

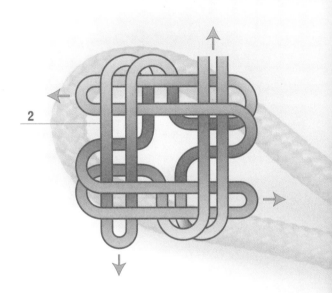

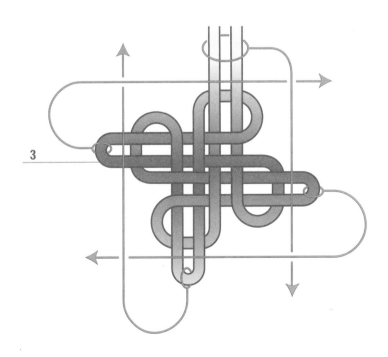

<46>

METHOD

Fold a cord in half and create three long loops (four, including the two standing ends) and crown the four doubled parts (figs. 1–2). Draw up snugly and then crown again, this time in the opposite direction (figs. 3–4). Tighten to produce alternating large and small loops (fig. 5). It looks even better with five parts (fig. 6).

4

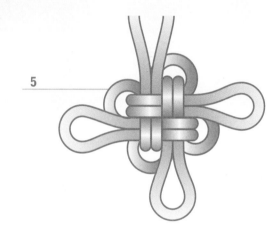

5

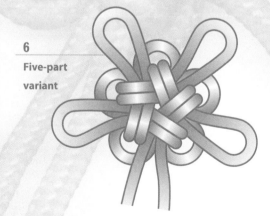

6

Five-part variant

HISTORY

This was a nameless orphan until Lydia Chen adopted and named it in 1981.

<47>

KNIFE LANYARD KNOT

APPLICATIONS

Originally used to form the loop of a neck lanyard that actually did have a seaman's knife suspended from it. This knot will do for anything requiring a fixed loop in a middled strand.

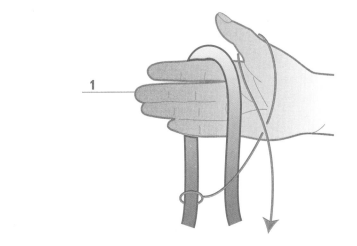

METHOD

There is a smooth way (figs. 1–2) to create the layout through which a locking tuck then passes U-O-U-O to form the flat knot (fig. 3) called a carrick bend. Tuck the two working ends around and up through the middle of the knot, as shown. Holding the loop in one hand, use the fingers of the other hand to stroke the knot gently down and away with the loop, to arrive at the round knot form (fig. 4). Tighten a bit at a time with fingers and then pliers (if necessary).

   For a bulkier knot, follow the original lead around a second time, making twin parallel knot parts (figs. 5–6). Then tighten (fig. 7). It will be necessary to pull each bit of slack around through the knot twice. Start at the loop (once it is the desired size) so that the accumulated bight can finally be pulled out of the knot without affecting the loop dimension.

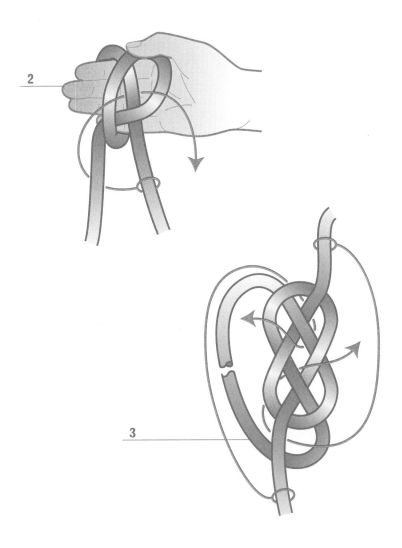

<48>

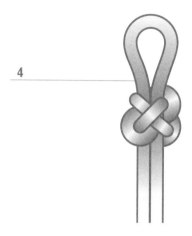

4

HISTORY

In the past this knot has also been called a two-strand diamond knot.

5

**Doubling
the original lead**

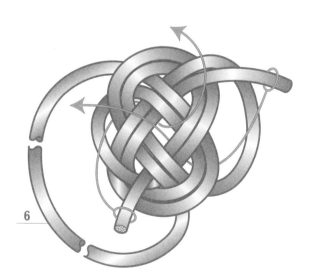

6

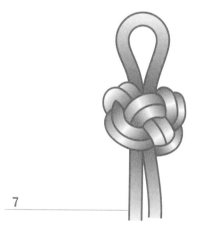

7

<49>

FOOTROPE KNOT

APPLICATIONS

Apart from the original use (see History opposite) that gave this knot its name, it rarely stands alone. It is a gathering knot and starting point for the button or globe knots, and the plaits and braids which are described later. This works best in three or more strands, when it creates a neat knot which will not slip and slide since it is an integral part of the cords in which it is tied. A footrope knot can be done with just two strands but it comes out as a somewhat puny thing.

METHOD

First tie a crown knot. Add a wall knot beneath it, with the working ends going in the same direction as the crown knot. Tuck the ends up through the centre of the knot as shown (fig. 1) and pull snug and tight (fig. 2). These instructions are summarized in the traditional nautical work rhyme:

> *First a crown,*
> *Then a wall.*
> *Tuck up,*
> *And that's all.*
> Capt. Charles W. Smith, c.1900

Once fluent with this knot, it is possible to merge the Wall-&-tuck into one movement, for which the updated mnemonic is:

> *Make a crown*
> *And cross one part.*
> *Then tuck the end*
> *Up through the heart.*
> John Smith[IGKT], Surrey, England, 1985

To double the footrope knot, follow the initial layout around with each working end in turn, tucking above original strands (figs. 3–4). Tighten methodically (fig. 5).

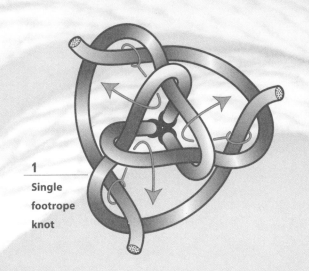

1
Single footrope knot

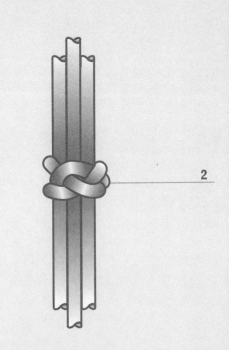

2

<50>

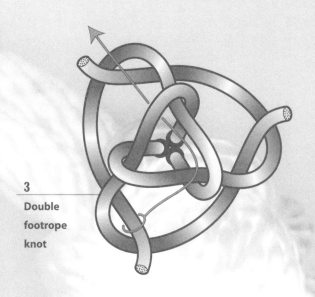

3

Double footrope knot

HISTORY

In the days of life under sail at sea, footropes were the ropes stretched beneath the yards and jib-booms, for men to stand on while loosing or furling the sails. A series of footrope knots provided a reassuring, slip-resistant extra foothold in that extremely precarious work-place.

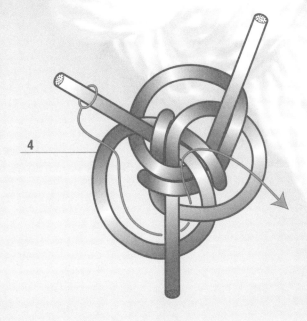

4

5

<51>

WALL KNOTS

APPLICATIONS

A single wall knot alone is not much use, but wall and crown knots (see p. 68) combine to create all kinds of button and globe knots.

METHOD

Two strands

If you can tie a solomon or bannister bar (see p. 142), then this basic version of a wall knot (figs. 1–2) will be nothing new; except that drawing it up snug requires a feel for how the knot wants to spread the tension evenly throughout itself. Despite the resulting interlocked kinks, however, note how both cords remain on their own side both entering and leaving the knot.

METHOD

Two strands (doubled)

For a more secure and bulkier knot, follow both initial leads around a second time (figs. 3–5).

3

Two strand (doubled) wall knot

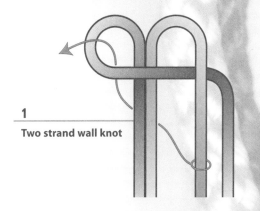

1

Two strand wall knot

4

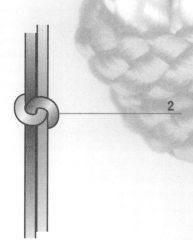

2

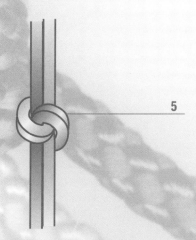

5

<52>

METHOD

Three (or more) strands

If you struggle unsuccessfully with a two-strand wall knot, you might find multi-strand versions (figs. 6–8) easier to understand, because – like crowning – the process is more repetitive in the multi-strand versions. Take care to keep the first bight open until you can secure it with the final locking tuck.

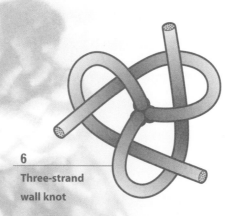

6

Three-strand wall knot

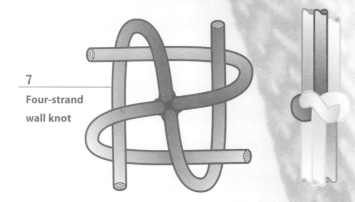

7

Four-strand wall knot

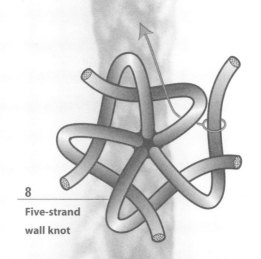

8

Five-strand wall knot

<53>

METHOD

Complex wall knot

When the knot must contract firmly around a foundation, try taking each strand under two (or more) other strands (fig. 9). The resulting knot (fig. 10) acts like the contractile iris of an eye or camera lens. These O-O-U-U (or O-O-O-U-U-U) wall knots are indispensable for ambitiously fancy knotwork.

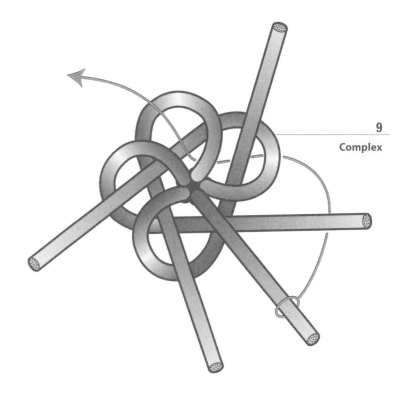

9
Complex

HISTORY

An old, and more appropriate, name for the wall knot was wale knot (a 'wale' being a raised ridge woven into a basket to strengthen it), which is perhaps why some knots based upon it then came to be known misleadingly as whale knots.

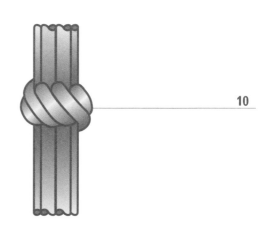

10

<54>

MATTHEW WALKER KNOTS

APPLICATIONS

These knots serve as stoppers in the end of lines to prevent them pulling out of whatever they may be put through. They also make compact, good-looking end knots. And Matthew Walker knots are used as dividers between different plaits, braids or hitches in long items of decorative knotwork, such as leashes, whips, and bellropes.

METHOD

Two-strand Matthew Walker knot
Tie a wall knot (figs. 1–2) and then tuck each end once more as shown (fig. 3). Now comes the tricky bit. Matthew Walker knots, more than any other knots I know, have to undergo a lot of internal twisting and sliding of moving knot parts before they settle down into their proper shape. The tension of one strand must exactly match that of the other. Note how – unlike the wall knot – the strands cross over within the knot (fig. 4), so that what enters on the left emerges on the right and vice-versa. This cross-over is essential for succesful tying of these knots. Once the knot tightens, although it is impossible to see, it is actually a couple of simple overhand or thumb knots interlinked and intertwined.

NOTE: It is advisable to become adept at a two-strand Matthew Walker knot before going on to tackle one with more strands.

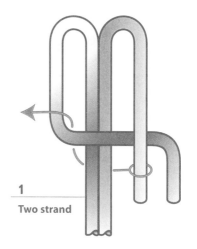

1
Two strand

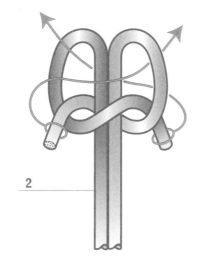

2

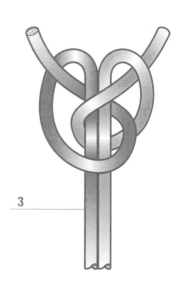

3

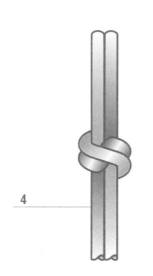

4

<55>

METHOD
Two-strand Matthew Walker knot (lengthened)

Make an extra couple of tucks (figs. 5–6) for a doubled knot, yet another couple for a trebled one (figs. 7–8), and exercise even more care in the way you let them wrap and slide into their finished forms.

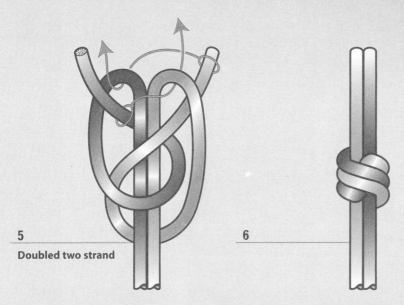

5

Doubled two strand

6

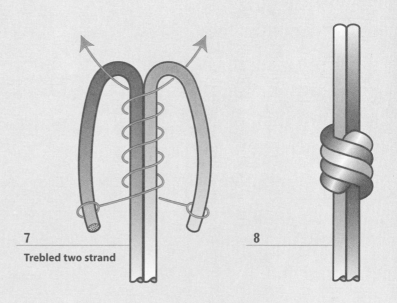

7

Trebled two strand

8

<56>

METHOD
Three (four or five) strand Matthew Walker knot

This hand-held method of directly tying these awkward knots (figs. 9–12) is not the only way, but it is perhaps the most easily pictured and remembered. It also clearly demonstrates the characteristic nature of interlocking overhand or thumb knots with each strand knotted around itself. Matching tension on all the strands is even more critical in pulling these knots snug and firm.

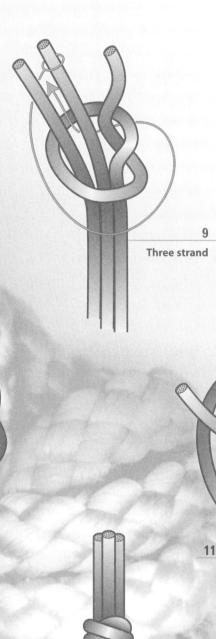

9

Three strand

10

11

12

<57>

METHOD

Complex Matthew Walker knot

To tie a Matthew Walker knot with any larger number of strands, seize the working strands to their foundation in three places and then conceal them by wrapping around with a piece of thick paper or other material. Now double the working strands back on themselves (fig. 13), seizing them in place, and then tuck each one in turn under one or two adjacent strands (fig. 14), at the same time loosening them so that they spiral as shown. Having completed one circuit of the growing knot, repeat the tucking process until each strand returns to the starting point and goes underneath itself (that is, ties an overhand or thumb knot in itself). Remove all but one of the inner seizings. Place an extra wrapper around the waist of the newly created knot (fig. 15), to hold everything in its place, and begin the painstaking business of drawing the knot parts snug (fig. 16). It is possible to build complex knots like this with less (or more) tucks than there are strands, but I feel that a Matthew Walker is not truly a Matthew Walker unless it is composed of interlocked overhand or thumb knots.

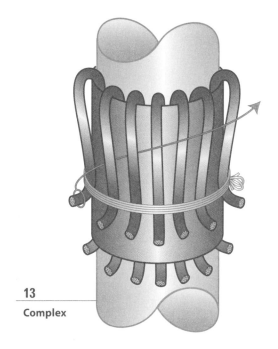

13

Complex

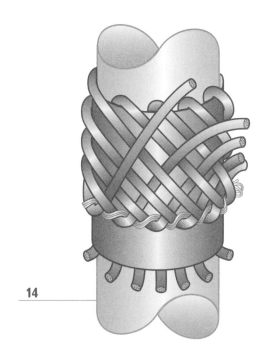

14

<58>

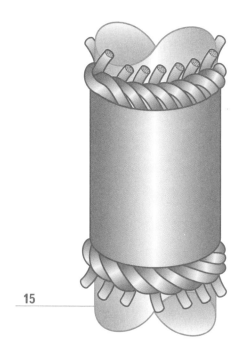

15

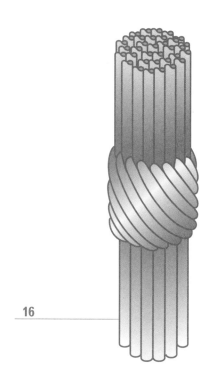

16

HISTORY

Darcy Lever wrote in 1808: "This is a handsome Knot for the end of a Laniard". And he called it Matthew Walker's knot, the apostrophe 's' causing some later commentators to assume that he must have known (or at least been aware of) the man who devised this remarkable knot. Nobody now knows who Matthew Walker was. In their 1896 seamanship manual Todd & Whall stated: "Amongst *knots proper* (my italics) the Matthew Walker is almost the only one which it is absolutely necessary for the seaman to know". They were referring, of course, to the strict definition of a knot (see **Glossary**) as one that appears only in the end of a rope. The rope handles (beckets) of deck and fire buckets aboard ships were supposed to be secured with a pair of Matthew Walker knots. When I was a sea cadet around 1950, my seamanship instructors were still repeating the (by then outmoded) dogma that this knot was "to put a becket in a bucket".

<59>

BUTTON KNOTS AND GLOBE KNOTS

Small and compact knotted buttons need no core to fill them; larger globe knots may do so, and indeed make handsome spherical coverings to swell the ends of barrier ropes and bell-ropes. They can also be used to add slip-resistant handgrips to tools, or to cover the knob of a manual gear change lever on a classic car.

Edge-detail of a 12-strand square knot

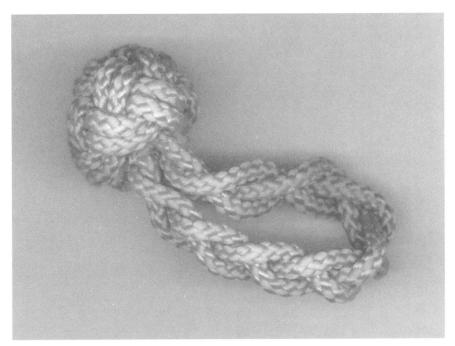

Doubled Chinese button

CHINESE BUTTON KNOTS

APPLICATIONS

Like so many fancy knots, this is a pleasure simply to make for its own sake, but it does create a basic button suitable for any occasion. Note that knotted buttons are often too big for buttonholes and so require cord loops to accommodate them.

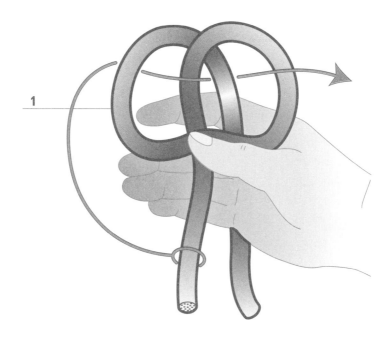

METHOD

Tie directly in the hand as shown here and overleaf (figs. 1–3). Draw up carefully to obtain a roughly spherical knob with the working ends as twin stems. Spot how the top central knot part (arrowed in fig. 4 on p.64) tends to recede beneath the surface. Before the final round of tightening, prick it up to the surface and trap it there.

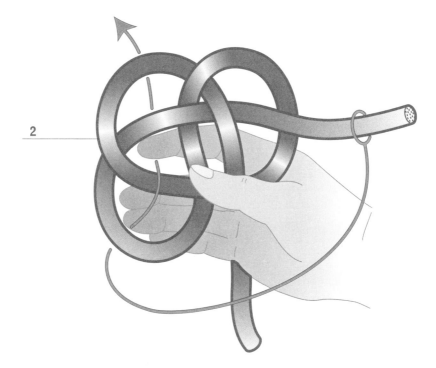

<63>

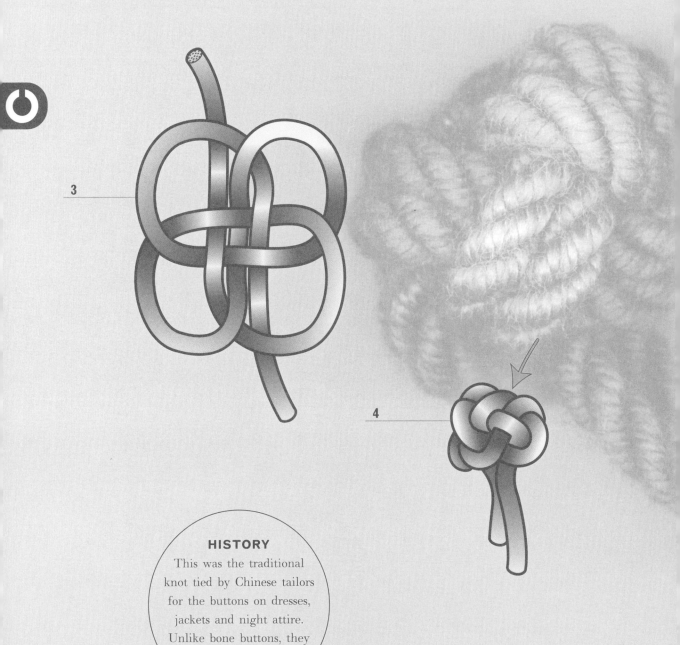

3

4

HISTORY

This was the traditional knot tied by Chinese tailors for the buttons on dresses, jackets and night attire. Unlike bone buttons, they were unbreakable.

<64>

METHOD
Doubled Chinese button knot

The Chinese button knot may be doubled (figs. 5–6), in which case it must be turned over prior to tightening so that the working ends project down. If this is done the centre will not sink down (fig. 7) as it is supported by an underlying knot part.

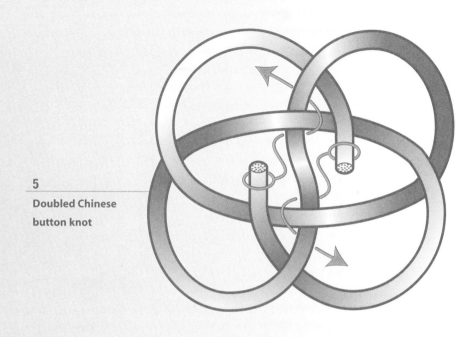

5

Doubled Chinese button knot

6

7

<65>

MANROPE KNOT

APPLICATIONS

Wherever a good-looking lump is needed on the end of a three- to five-strand rope or braid, this knot will fill the role.

METHOD

First make a wall knot, then add a crown on top of it (figs. 1–2). Ensure that the working ends continue in the same direction; in other words both wall and crown should go anti-clockwise (as in the example illustrated) or both clockwise. Follow the original lead, parallel to (and below) it, with each working end in turn, and finally tuck each working end down through the knot as shown (fig. 3). Tighten all round to create the button-like knob (fig. 4). This knot can often be trebled and still look good. The traditional and anonymous work rhyme for this knot is:

> *First a wall,*
> *And then a crown.*
> *Next tuck up,*
> *And then tuck down.*

NOTE: In doubling many compound knots, the recommended route is above the original lead, but in the case of the manrope knot, it is quite obvious from the way the single crown knot sits atop its underlying wall knot that this is an exception to that guideline. Indeed, it is generally best to go where the knot wants to go.

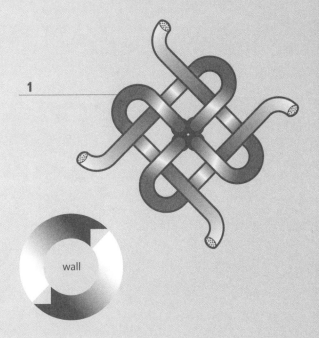

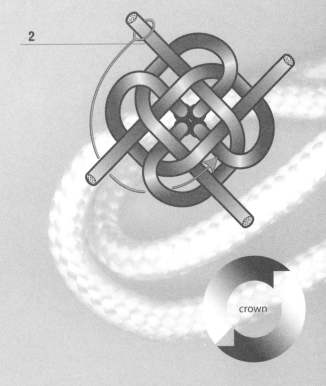

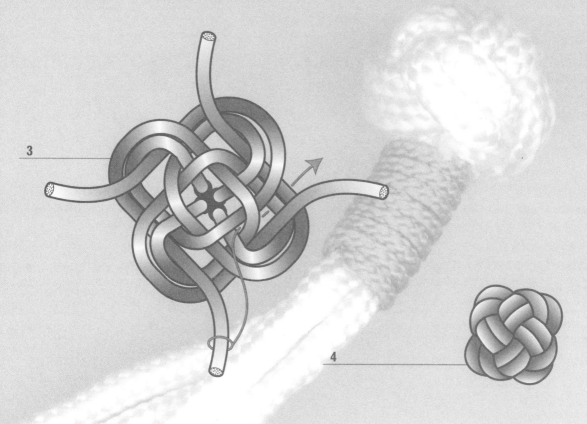

HISTORY

Used as a handhold for passenger boarding ladder ropes, the 18th-century name for this knot was 'double Wall and double Crown', or occasionally, for a different purpose, it was called the 'Topsail Halyard Sheet Knot'. In 1804, Norie's naval dictionary called it a 'Kop Knot' and then Wm. N. Brady in 1841 used its present name. Exactly a century later Albert Wetjen wrote: "A man who can tie a Manrope Knot… is an object of respect".

<67>

STAR KNOT

APPLICATIONS

This good-looking knot is a great favourite with decorative knot tyers who use it as a middle or end knot whenever possible.

METHOD

A star knot can be tied with three or four strands but looks best in five or perhaps six strands. Take it step-by-step and it is a simple but satisfying knot to create. The base is a wall knot made of underhand loops (fig. 1). Crown in the opposite direction (fig. 2) and tuck each strand back underneath itself. Both of these stages can, with practise, be done in one movement. Parallel the original lead with each working end in turn, which then dives down through the corner compartments. By now the knot is taking shape (fig. 3). Tuck the ends, one by one, through the underside as shown (fig. 4) to emerge once again at the top (fig. 5) in the centre. Left like this, it would be a lanyard knot. However, if you tuck each working end in turn back down through four knot parts (fig. 5) a neat button knot is made (fig. 6). Alternatively, single or double crown the ends prior to tucking them, for a crowned star knot (fig. 7).

1

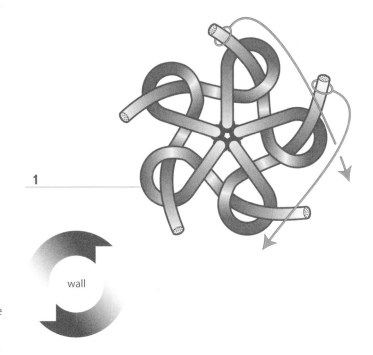

wall

2

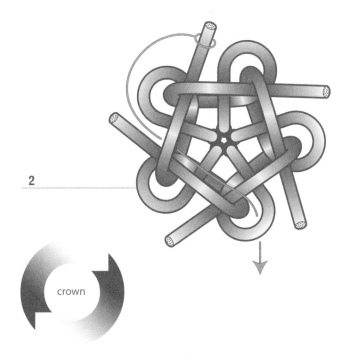

crown

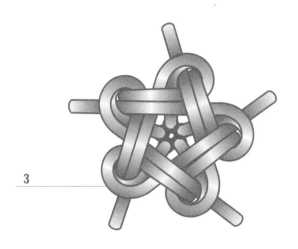

3

5

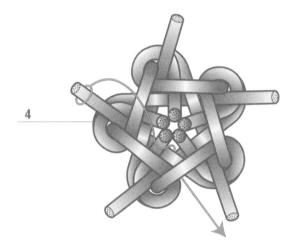

4

6

HISTORY

This knot is often said to be
unique in that it is unlike any
other knot in its construction, but, to
my mind, it is another wall-&-crown
compound knot, albeit an imaginative
one. References to it appear in the
19th century and the first
illustration seems to have been
by E. N. Little (1889).

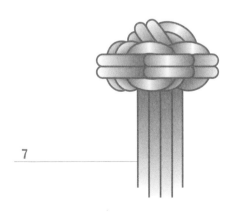

7

<69>

PLANET EARTH

APPLICATIONS

One of the smaller spherical coverings, it will mould itself to any kind of small ball or bead for decoration or as a slip- or wear-resistant grip.

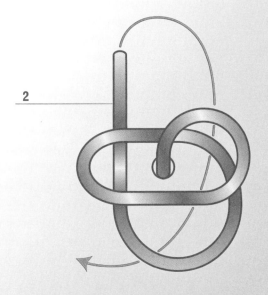

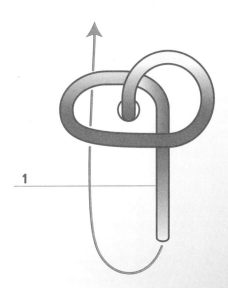

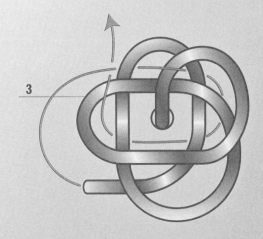

METHOD

Take a single strand and, following the lead as indicated (figs. 1–4), pin it onto a base over a drawing of the final layout (fig. 5), or simply hold it down on a flat surface. Remove any pins, taking care not to disturb the layout, and place the knot over the core to be covered. Work it to shape, pulling out slack. Follow the original lead around with the working end to double, treble or quadruple the knot. Bury the two ends.

<70>

4

5

HISTORY

Clifford Ashley stated that this knot was original (implying that he devised it) and referred to it merely as a spherical covering. It is knot number 2216 in *The Ashley Book of Knots*, where he also wrote (not specifically about this knot): "It is hardly necessary to name a knot, but it assists materially in finding it a second time if the occasion arises". So I have named this one and, as it is not perfectly spherical but is flattened at the poles and wider around the equator (in other words, it is like our world, an oblate spheroid), I have called it Planet Earth. The next three covering knots – also Ashley originals – I have consequently named in increasing order of size: Uranus, Saturn and Jupiter.

<71>

URANUS

APPLICATIONS

This covering knot is a scaled-up version of the planet earth knot on pages 70–1.

METHOD

Take a single strand and pin it out, in the same manner as the planet earth knot, over a drawing of the completed layout. Bring the working end out alongside the standing end prior to doubling the knot.

1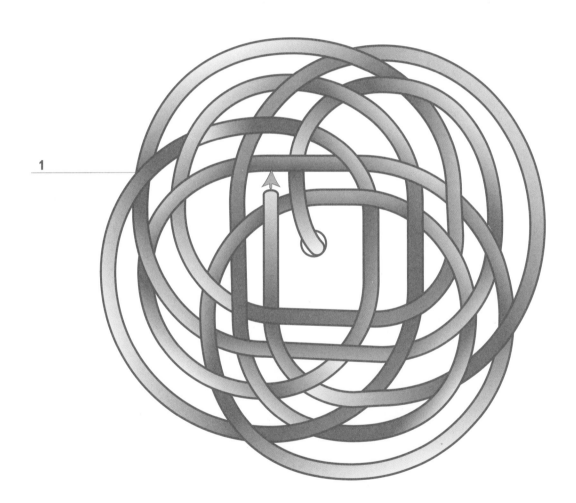

<72>

SATURN

APPLICATIONS

This knot, like Jupiter on page 74, will make a handsome, slip-resistant and protective cover for any round object. With a fine, attractive cord, a tiny marble and patience, you can create an unusual earring or charm bracelet accessory. Using a thicker rope around something the size of a modest cannon ball, you could produce an excellent door stop (one that remains where placed due to its own inertia, but that can be readily rolled aside with one push from a foot). In between sizes can be used on the ends of curtain tie-backs or light pulls, barrier and bell-ropes.

METHOD

First locate a point about one third along the cord from the standing end and work from there onwards (fig. 1), as it will be necessary to double, treble or quadruple the knot (fig. 2) in both directions (using standing and working ends). It is crucial to have two more or less equal working lengths. This knot (fig. 1), like the next one, seems to be flawed in one place where the lead goes under two consecutive crossing points. Then, when it is tightened up all round, the apparent blemish in the O-U-O-U will recede beneath the surface – provided the ball, bead or other filling is placed beneath the knot as it appears on the page.

1

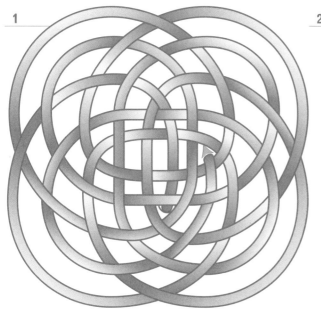

2

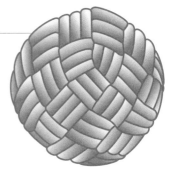

HISTORY

Uranus, Saturn and Jupiter knots are scaled-up versions of Ashley originals (see History, p.71).

<73>

JUPITER

APPLICATIONS

See the preceding three knots on pages 70–3. While great care and caution must be exercised over what is given to any pet animal, I have seen this knot tied over a croquet ball as a dog's plaything and, after several years of being gnawed and soaked in canine saliva, it remained in sound condition. I do not recommend it for this purpose but it just shows how robust knotwork can be in the right circumstances.

METHOD

Refer to the preceding knots on pages 70–3. Like Saturn, this knot too has an apparent O-U-U-O flaw and must also be doubled by following the initial lead around with both working end and standing end. It draws up naturally as a prolate spheroid (narrower at its equator than between its poles).

1

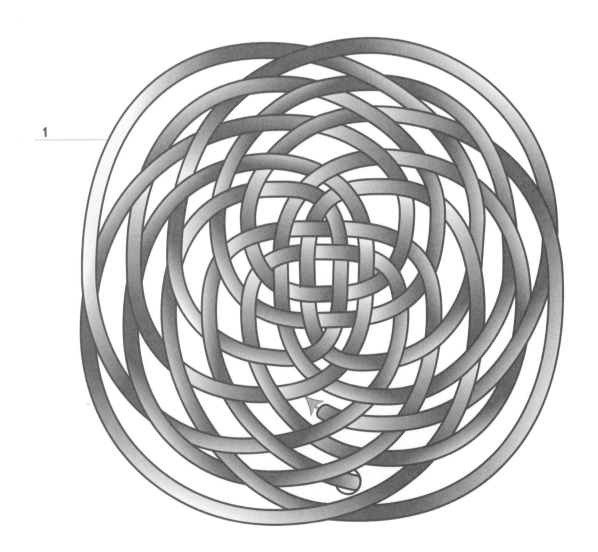

<74>

SIX-STRAND ROUND KNOT

APPLICATIONS

Use it as a handsome button, stopper or globe knot.

METHOD

Tie a wall knot with six strands (fig. 1). If these strands are secured around a fairly thick foundation, then a single wall knot may be just right. For a thinner core, try a knot which tucks under two or three rim bights. Now imagine the wall knot is covered over with a sheet of stiff paper or card. Indeed, you may actually want to do this at first – later you will not bother. Tie the specially interlaced crown knot as illustrated (fig. 2). Both knots have the same handedness or polarity, circling anti-clockwise in this example. Double the lead and tighten the knot.

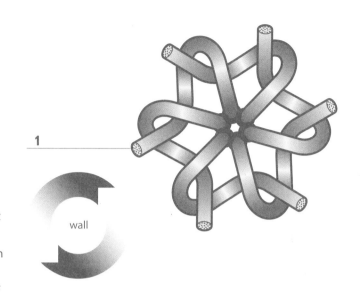

1

wall

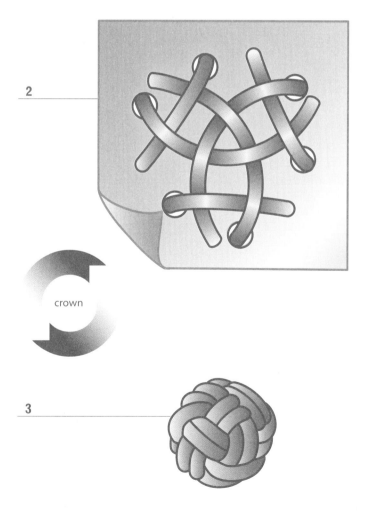

2

crown

3

<75>

EIGHT-STRAND ROUND KNOT

APPLICATIONS

More or less round button or globe knots may be made with virtually any number of strands, which are crowned on top of a suitable wall knot, and doubled or trebled to fill in the spaces between the initial lead.

 1

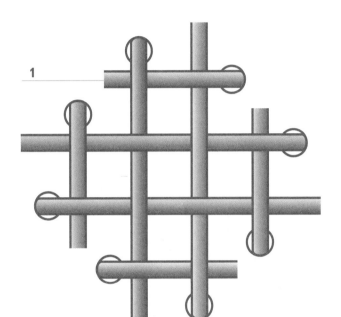

wall   crown

METHOD

Just one round knot is illustrated – tied with eight strands – which results in a shape that is more square than anything. It requires purposeful but patient tightening to achieve the final form; and, in common with all such knots using over six strands, it may also need a piece of stiff card or such-like (in this instance cut round) to retain the shape suggested by the particular crown knot.

HISTORY

This crown knot was first illustrated by Alston in 1860, although inventive interweaving of multi-strand crown knots no doubt arose much earlier.

<76>

SQUARE KNOTS

APPLICATIONS

Get away from the ubiquitous round knot with this square one. It makes a handsome button.

METHOD

Eight-strand square knot

See the preceding two knots for details, but note that for this knot, wall and crown are reversed in order to achieve the best possible square appearance.

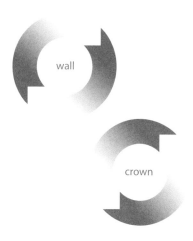

wall

crown

METHOD

Twelve-strand square knot

See the previous three knots on pages 74–6. Wall and crown in opposite directions (fig. 3). Double or treble around a core as necessary (fig. 4).

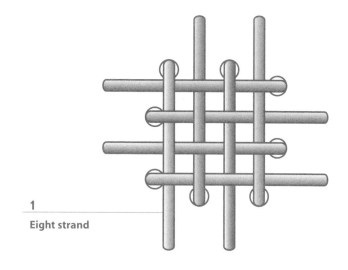

1

Eight strand

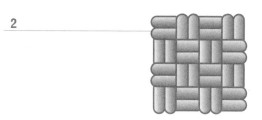

2

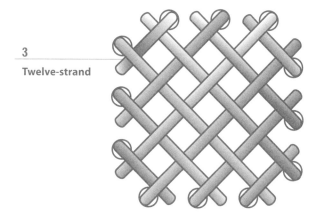

3

Twelve-strand

4

<77>

TEN-STRAND ROUND KNOT

APPLICATIONS

Big strands make big knots but multi-strand button and globe knots may be kept small by using finer cords. This knot can end a plaited key fob, up-&-over garage door lanyard, rudder-lines on a traditional rowing wherry, or anything else circumstances and your imagination can contrive. Then again, it is satisfying merely to tie for its own sake.

METHOD

See the preceding knots on pages 75–7. Wall and crown (fig. 1) in the same direction, doubling (fig. 2) or trebling for a handsome, symmetrical finish around a core.

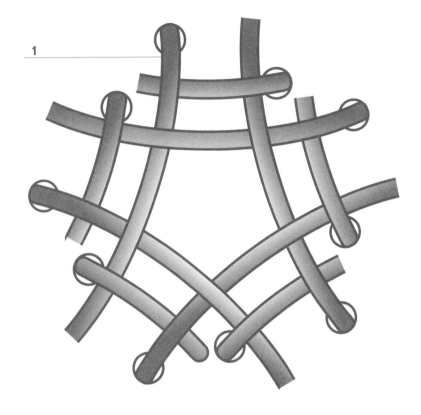

1

wall

crown

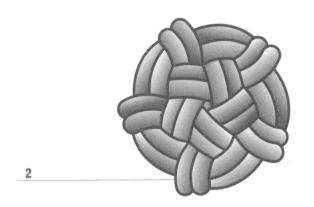

2

<78>

BULKIER GLOBE KNOTS

Variations on the preceding knots may be made by trying out other crown knots of your own devising, as well as experimenting with changing the direction of walls and crowns. The best knots – those that tend to find a favoured place in any knot tyer's repertoire – are generally the ones with a shape that is easy to achieve. Nonetheless, some others (from triangles and rectangles to pentagons and even heart-shapes) can be as good, if patience and care are taken in tensioning them; pounding them with a mallet or the thick end of a fid can work wonders.

You will discover that four-sided gaps between panels of knot parts are ideal (fig. 2). Triangular ones close up nicely (fig. 3), but they may not always remain neat when doubled and (especially) trebled. Five-sided spaces (fig. 5) should be avoided, if at all possible, as they will let a bit of the underlying core show through to disfigure the finished work.

Enormous knots are needed to cover the biggest cores and these require an extra technique. Leave a gap between the wall and crown; rotate them in opposite directions so that their common standing parts helix (fig. 1) and tuck each working end in turn O-U-O to fill in the space between the other two knots. Turn around by means of a second wall beside (outside of) the first one. Here is a tip. If the first wall was O-O-O-U-U-U, then make its neighbour merely O-O-U-U, and the third one simply O-U.

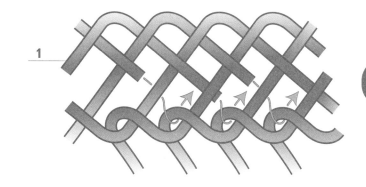

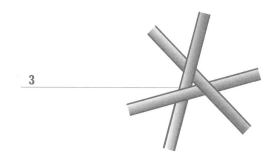

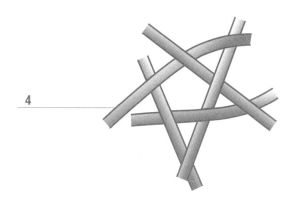

<79>

TURK'S HEAD

I've always thought that the Turk's head's beauty,
range of usefulness, and elegant mathematical
underpinnings qualified it as a miraculous knot.
Brion Toss[IGKT], master rigger, Brooklin, Maine, USA, 1984

0

The Turk's head is the ultimate decorative – yet wholly practical – knot and its almost limitless variations are subject only to the amount of cord available and the knot tyer's ability, patience and tenacity. It is so named because the knots were once thought to resemble turbans. Detailed instruction manuals have been written entirely about the mathematics and tying techniques of the various branches of this massive family of knots, and some people devote all of their knot tying exclusively to Turk's heads. These intricate knots are wrongly assumed to be the exclusive products of sailors aboard square-rigged clippers, whalers and windjammers. However, leather braiders, including western American cowboys, tied Turk's heads every bit as complex (and they were bequeathed them by the earlier Spanish vaqueros from South America).

While it is possible to tie Turk's heads with more than one strand, devotees derive the greatest satisfaction from those that can be tied in a single cord, and all those included in this book can be tied that way. Turk's heads are described by two dimensions (see fig. 1), which are:

- the number of plaited parts or leads

- the number of scallop-shaped overlapping rim parts known as bights

The example shown (fig. 1 on p.83) has four leads (L) or parts and a number of bights (B), which cannot be known for certain as they disappear out of sight around the back of the illustration. There may be three, in which case this would be a 4L x 3B Turk's head, or perhaps five, making it a 4L x 5B knot. To be tied in a single cord, however, it cannot be a 4L x 4B, because of the Law of the Common Divisor (see opposite page).

Knots with just one bight more or less than the number of leads are referred to as 'square' Turk's heads. They are bracelets or collars of interwoven strands, which may also be flattened into circular mats. Tube-like ones with many more leads than bights are said to be 'long', and those with a lot more bights than leads form 'narrow' braided strips.

A 5L x 4B Turk's head

<82>

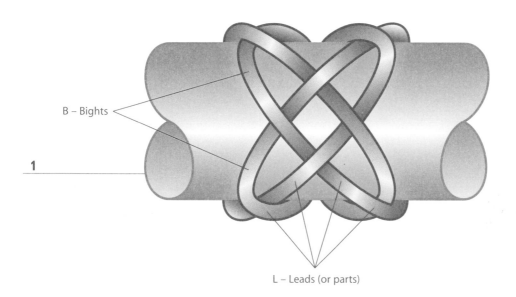

B – Bights

1

L – Leads (or parts)

THE LAW OF THE COMMON DIVISOR

The discovery of this empirical rule is jointly credited to Clifford W. Ashley and George H. Taber (with whom Ashley was corresponding as early as 1916). Quite simply a Turk's head cannot be completed with a single cord if the number of its leads and bights can be divided by a common number. So a 3 x 3, 3 x 6 or 3 x 9 single-strand Turk's head is impossible, because in every instance the two dimensions divide by 3 (the common divisor). They can be tied, but not with a single cord. Other impossible single-strand Turk's heads include a 4 x 4 (both divide by 2 and 4), 5 x 5 (both divide by 5), 6 x 6 (both divide by 3 and 6) and 6 x 9 (both divide by 3). But a 3L x 4B (or a 3B x 4L) knot is possible, and so is a 3 x 5 or a 3 x 7.

Mathematical proof did not appear until the spring of 1991, when an article by J.C. Turner[IGKT] with A.G. Shaake, both of the University of Waikato, Hamilton, New Zealand, was published in Issue No. 35 of *Knotting Matters*.

THE RULE OF THE GREATEST COMMON FACTOR

In September 1997, Jesse Coleman[IGKT] of Alabama, USA, published in *Knotting Matters* his modified rule which actually reveals how many cords will be needed for any Turk's head. For example, take a 9B x 6L (or a 6B x 9L – it makes no difference), 9 divides by 1, 3 and 9, and the factors of 6 are 1, 2, 3 and 6. The greatest factor common to both numbers is 3; therefore 3 cords will be required to tie either of these Turk's heads. Where there appears to be no common divisor, as in single-strand knots, the greatest common factor is actually 1 (and so one strand is all that is needed).

<83>

2L X 3B

APPLICATIONS

This unusual, twined Turk's head is rarely seen, yet such a simple embellishment may sometimes be more eye-catching than an elaborate one. Use it to embellish the rims of indoor plant pots or waste paper bins and baskets, and try it in place of any three- or four-part narrow Turk's head.

METHOD

Tie a half knot around the item to be embraced, taking the working end around a second time and tucking it as shown (fig. 1). Then merely follow the original lead, parallel to it, matching its U-O-U sequence (figs. 2–4) until a two-ply knot results. Treble it (fig. 5) if you like.

NOTE: A single initial twining tuck will make a 2L x 3B version of the knot; two tucks will result in a 2L x 5B; three tucks a 2L x 7B; four tucks, 2L x 9B; and so on.

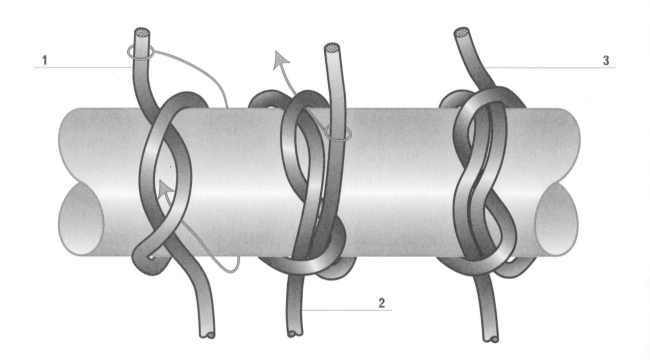

<84>

0

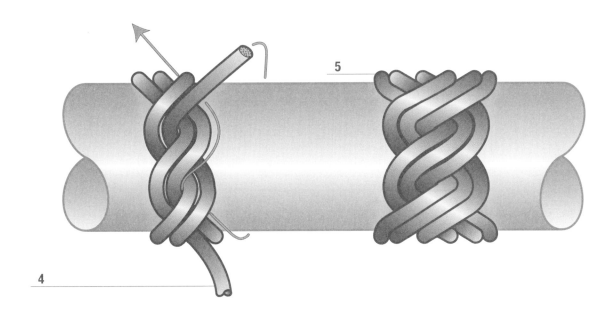

5

4

<85>

3L X 4 (OR MORE) B

APPLICATIONS
The 3L x 4B square Turk's head makes a sliding clasp for a neckerchief; indeed, it is the oddly named 'woggle' traditionally worn by uniformed Scouts. It may also be used for items as diverse as serviette rings, candle holders, or drip rings for canoe paddles. Tied in rope it will stop a terracotta plant pot from blowing over in a gale.

METHOD
Take a couple of turns around either hand (figs. 1 or 2). Mentally label the nearest end (hanging down in front) as the working end, and the furthest one (off the back of the hand) the standing end. With the working end begin a three-strand plait (fig. 3). If in doubt, refer to Plaits and Braids, page 140. Pull the working end free from the bottom of the half-completed knot, and tuck it O-U-O-U as shown (fig. 4). Rotate the knot carefully until you can see the working end and standing end close together on the same side. Tuck the standing end alongside the working end (fig. 5). Follow the original lead around with either end to double or triple the knot. Tighten it with fingers and pliers in the usual way.

Continue plaiting to form a Turk's head every time the working end and standing end emerge on the same side of the knot. Starting, as here, with the working end will produce 3L x 1B (4B, 7B, etc.) knots. Picking up the standing end first results in 3L x 2B (5B, 8B, etc.) knots. From these two starts, any size of 3L narrow Turk's head can be made.

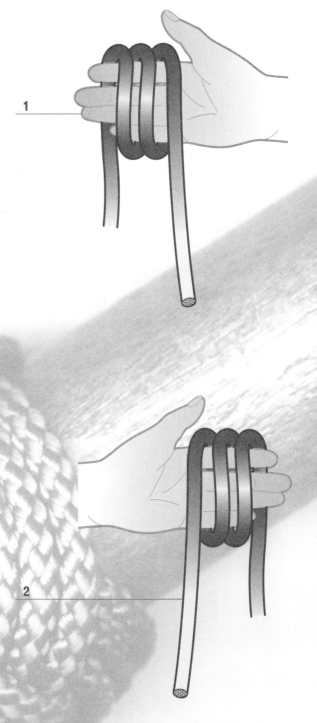

1

2

<86>

It may be that each new
generation of avid Turk's head fans
rediscovers this plaiting method of
tying three-lead knots. Clifford Ashley did.
And so too did Brian Field[IGKT], professional
quayside knot tyer at Maldon in Essex,
England, to the delight of summer tourists.
He has used it to teach, with equal
success, Scout leaders at an
international jamboree and a class
of six-year-olds in a
primary school.

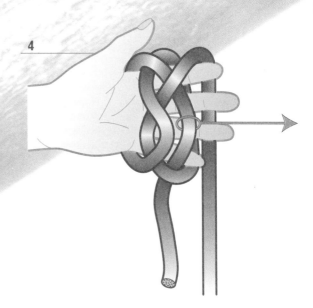

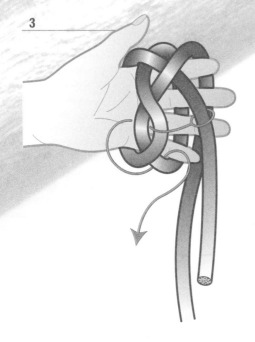

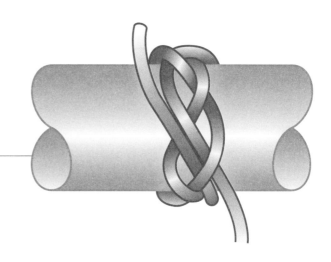

<87>

RAISING A 3L X 4B SQUARE TURK'S HEAD TO LARGER DIMENSIONS

APPLICATIONS
Square Turk's heads of various dimensions make secure permanent bindings.

METHOD
Tie a single-ply 3L x 4B Turk's head (fig. 1) and rearrange both standing and working ends to create a ladder of irregular U-U and O-O knot parts (fig. 2), as indicated by the diagonal line. Hold the knot to prevent this ladder disappearing, which it will do if the working end is allowed to slip back to its original position.

Rotate the work in your hand and tuck the working end from left to right as shown (fig. 3), making another ladder of irregularly tucked knot parts. Take the working end around and back to tuck alongside the standing end.

The tricky bit is now done and the satisfying stage begins. Make a locking tuck, from right to left, going O-U-O-U. Turn the working end and go from left to right in a second locking tuck O-U-O-U, then take the working end around a final time to be tucked alongside the standing end. Double and triple as desired.

The resulting knot is a 5L x 6B (adding two leads and two bights to the original dimensions). Repeating the process would produce a 7L x 8B and so on. Ladders and locking tucks (with regular O-U sequences) are reliable indicators of correctly laid out Turk's heads.

HISTORY
It appears that sailors and gauchos, who may have known only a few basic Turk's head starts (tied directly in the hand), made larger knots from smaller ones in this way; whereas contemporary Turk's head practitioners, with their extra know-how and resources, can tie large knots from scratch.

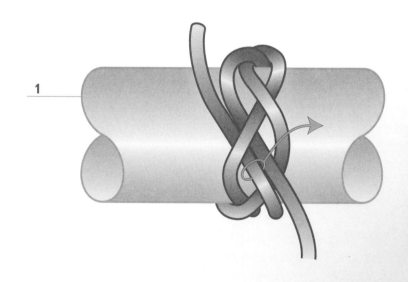

1

<88>

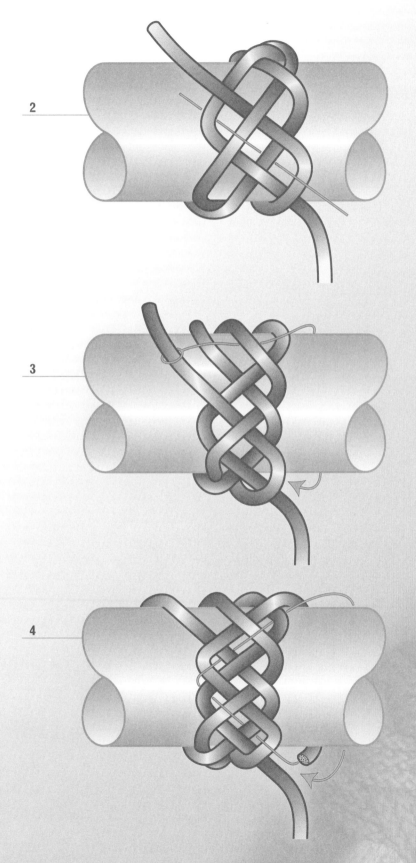

<89>

4L X 3B

APPLICATIONS

As for other square Turk's heads.

METHOD

Start with a simple overhand or thumb knot (fig. 1). Bring the end down around the back of the core and back up in front to split the starting knot (fig. 2) and create an OO-UU ladder of knot parts, before tucking O-U from right to left. Take the working end around again and tuck O-U-O (fig. 3), then bring the working end alongside the standing end (fig. 4) to double and treble the knot as desired.

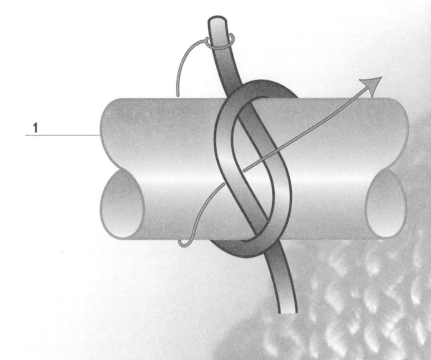

1

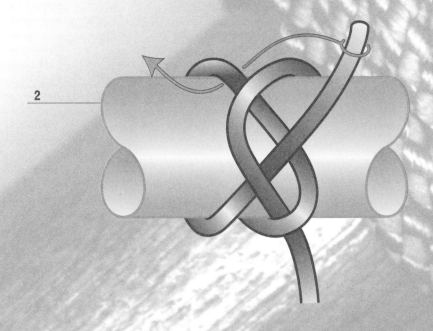

2

<90>

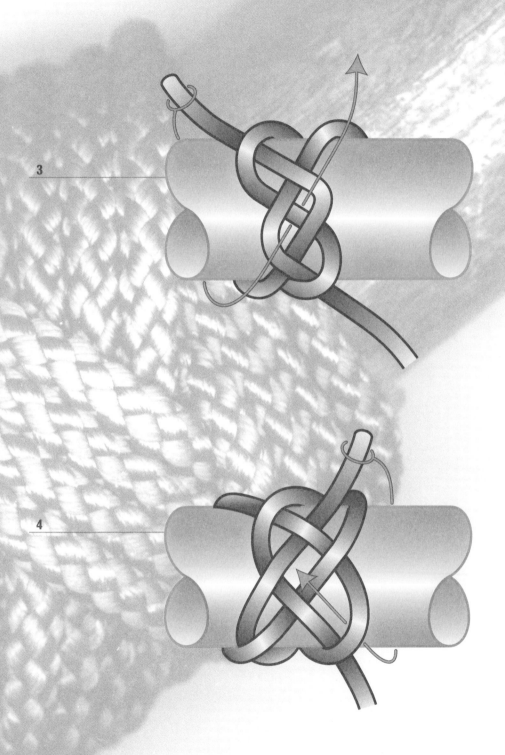

3

4

<91>

4L X 5B

APPLICATIONS

With its increased number of bights, this knot fits larger core diameters.

METHOD

It seems natural, as bights are added to square Turk's heads, to hold them in place by inserting fingers. Follow the lead shown (figs. 1–3), taking care to reproduce the O-U sequence exactly. Turk's heads, with their numerous crossing points, will not fall apart if one 'under' is mistakenly made 'over', but the appearance of the completed knot will be unacceptably marred by it. Having inserted the working end alongside the standing end, remove the knot from the fingers (fig. 4), slide it onto the foundation (fig. 5), double, treble and tighten.

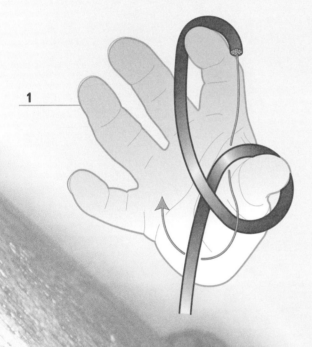

1

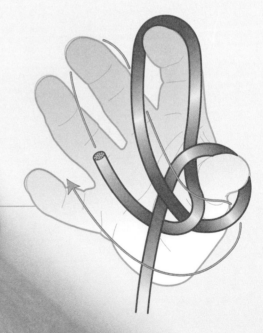

2

<92>

3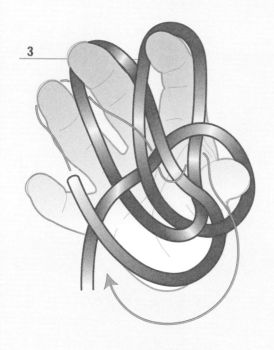

0

4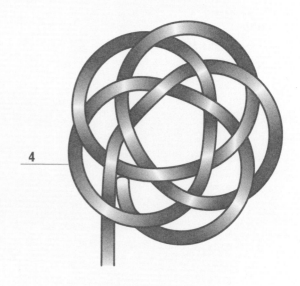

HISTORY

This finger-tying method – an excellent teaching aid – has been extensively demonstrated and written about since the early 1980s by the ingenious Charlie Smith[IGKT] of Chelmsford, Essex.

5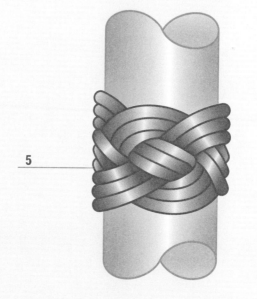

<93>

SIMPLE T-SHAPE

APPLICATIONS

When hitching or otherwise covering a wheel or handrail, occasional T-junctions intervene to leave unsightly gaps. This modified 4L x 5B Turk's head fills them.

METHOD

Tie a simple overhand or thumb knot (fig. 1), taking the working end down the back, then up and across to split the overhand knot as shown. Continue as illustrated (figs. 2–5) and bring the working end alongside the standing end (fig. 6). The single-ply knot is skimpy and barely adequate, but it bulks satisfactorily when doubled and trebled.

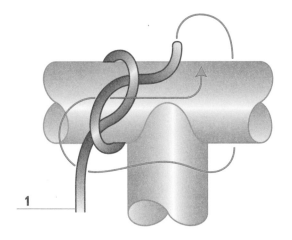

1

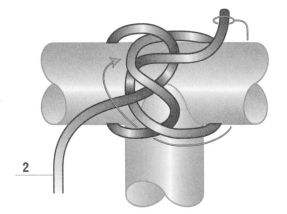

2

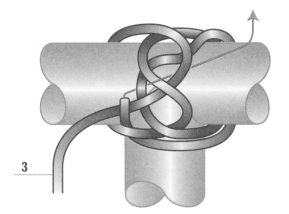

3

<94>

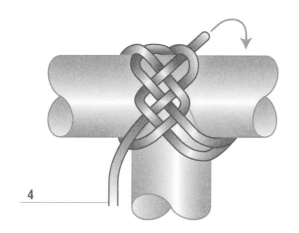

4

HISTORY

American rigger Brion Toss published this knot in 1984; but – I confess – I ignored it until 2nd November 1997, when that doyen of IGKT founder-members Frank Harris sat me down in a knotting workshop he was conducting at the National Motorboat Museum at Pitsea, in Essex, England, and made me learn it.

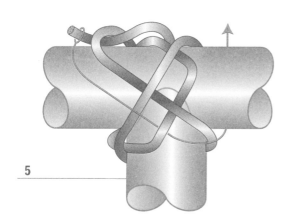

5

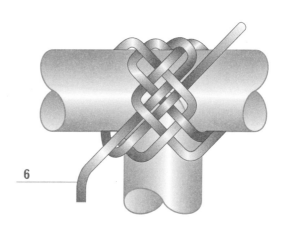

6

<95>

4L X 7B

APPLICATIONS
Use it when a knot slightly broader than a 3L narrow Turk's head is needed.

METHOD
A basic 4L x 3B Turk's head begins with a simple overhand or thumb knot, so a multi-bight version stems from a multiple overhand knot. Tie a double overhand knot, bring the working end around and split the twined knot as shown (fig. 1), making a series of locking tucks (figs. 2–4). Bring the working end alongside the standing end (fig. 5), before following the knot around.

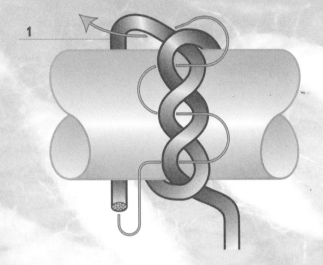

1

HISTORY
The principle of ply-splitting multiple overhand knots to produce 4L multi-bight Turk's heads was described by Frans Masurel[IGKT] and illustrated by Pieter van de Griend[IGKT] (both of the Netherlands) in the December 1995 issue of *Knotting Matters*.

<96>

2

3

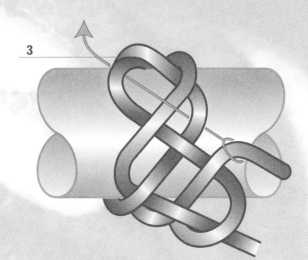

O

4

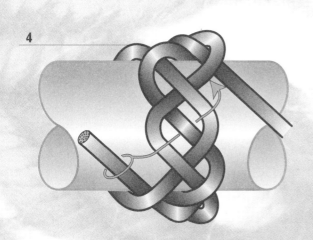

5

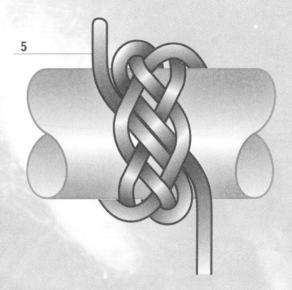

<97>

5L X 4B

APPLICATIONS
This is an intermediate square Turk's head that can easily be learnt and tied in the hand. I use them instead of simple whippings to prevent the ropes' ends aboard my sailing dinghy from fraying.

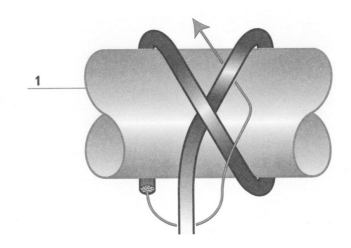

METHOD
The initial wrapping and tucking (figs. 1–2) creates two ladders, alongside which locking tucks (figs. 4–5) are subsequently made.

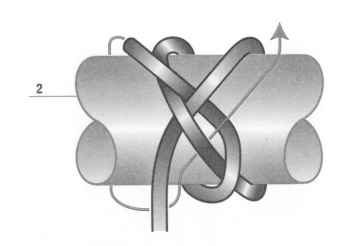

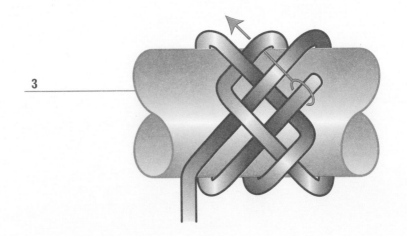

<98>

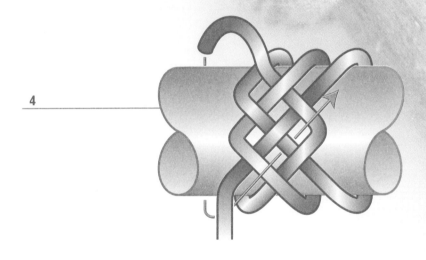

4

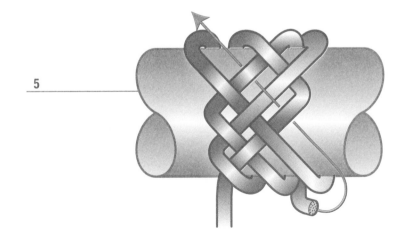

5

<99>

MÖBIUS BAND

APPLICATIONS

I contend that every knot has a use and that decorative knots are practical ones which also happen to look good. But even I have to ask, what use is a Möbius band Turk's head? It is at present an intellectual curiosity, done for its own sake, but some practical application may yet turn up.

METHOD

The original Möbius band was a strip of paper or other material that had been cut (fig. 1), one of the two ends was then rotated through 180° and rejoined (fig. 2). This shape has at least two extraordinary properties. If you begin to paint or colour along one side of it, then when you eventually return to the start you will have coloured both sides without having to lift your brush or crayon. The sole conclusion possible is that a Möbius band has only one side and only one edge.

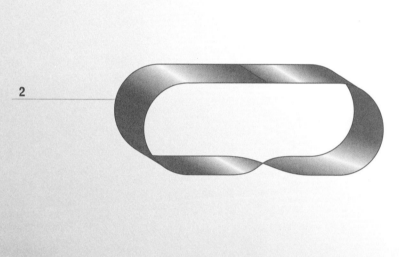

<100>

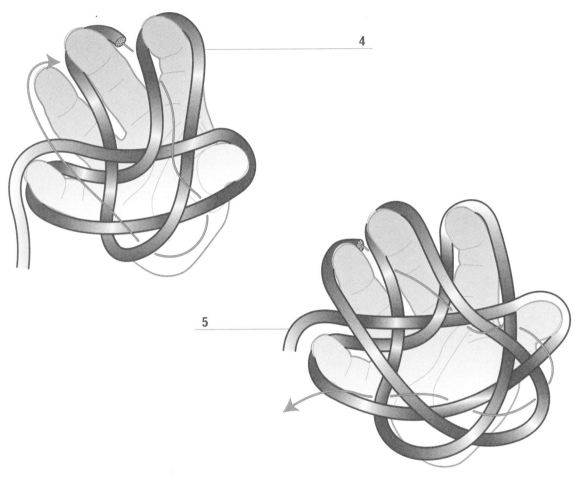

4

5

0

To tie just one of the many possible Möbius band Turk's heads, take a piece of cord about 2m (2yd) long, half it and arrange as shown (fig. 3) with the middle by the little finger. If you prefer to use your left hand, there is no need to reverse the diagrams; just remember that what is shown going around a thumb must go around your little finger (and vice versa). Create the exact O-U-O sequence (figs. 3–5). Next, carefully remove the almost completed knot from your hand and lay it on a flat surface. Rearrange the layout where both ends emerge from the knot by gently pulling out the bight indicated (fig. 6). Withdraw the working end from under its last crossing point (fig. 7) and re-tuck it alongside the standing end. Now follow the original lead around, doubling amd trebling the knot, when it will reveal the typical Möbius band form. This is a 4L knot with 14B (counting around its single edge).

<101>

6

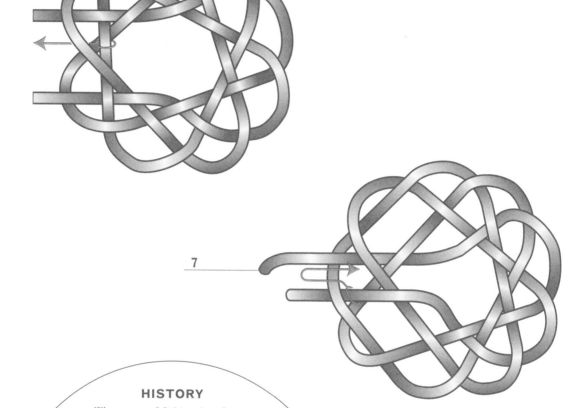

7

HISTORY

The paper Möbius band was discovered in 1858 by Augustus Ferdinand Möbius, the German mathematician and astronomer. Then, in February 1990, Dr John Turner[IGKT] and Georg Schaake, at the University of Waikato in Hamilton, New Zealand, produced an informal note (published five months later in Issue No. 32 of *Knotting Matters*) announcing their discovery of how to tie Möbius band Turk's heads and challenging IGKT members to tie some of the simpler ones. The authors included a picture of a 6L x 64B specimen they had made. Guild members who met the challenge and went on to explain and popularize them included Jane Kennedy, Europa Chang Dawson, Frank Harris and Charlie Smith.

<102>

16L X 3B

APPLICATIONS

Long Turk's heads – of which this is merely one example – make excellent handgrips to rail, spar, rope and tools, being slip-resistant and sweat-absorbent. But like many Turk's heads, they are also tied as fascinating puzzles.

METHOD

Wrap the working end, from left to right, three times down around the back of the foundation (fig. 1). Return, from right to left, tucking U-O-U-O-U (figs. 2a–2b). Reverse direction again, going parallel and to the left of the original lead but with opposite tucks O-U-U-O-O-U-U-O-O (the existing rim part, figs. 3a–3b). Note how changes of direction, with the exception of final locking tucks, generally have two consecutive tucks the same (i.e. a working end that emerges from the knot over will re-enter it over, and vice versa). Return, right to left, to the right of, and tucking opposite to, the previous lead O-U-U-O-O-U-U-O-O (trapping the standing end) -U (the rim part) (figs. 4a–4b). Make a final trip (L to R) with a series of locking tucks: U-O-O-U-U-O-O-U-U-O (rim part); and return (R to L), finishing with the locking sequence U-O-U-O-U-O-U-O-U-O-U-O-U-O-U (figs. 5a–5b). Bring the working end alongside the standing end, double, treble and tighten.

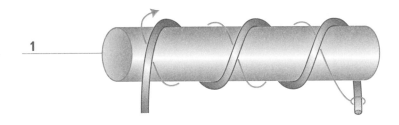

1

2a
Front

2b
Back

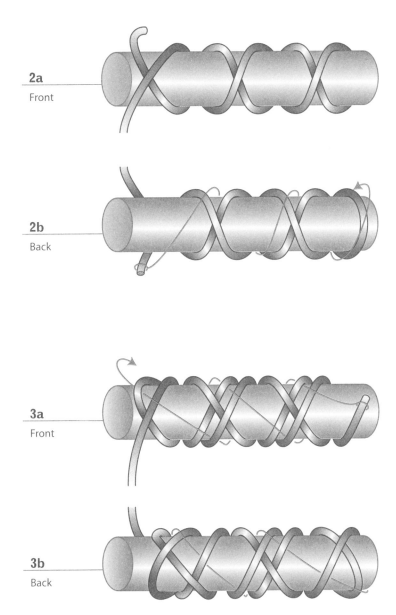

3a
Front

3b
Back

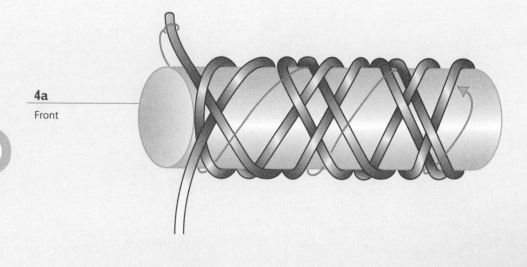

4a

Front

0

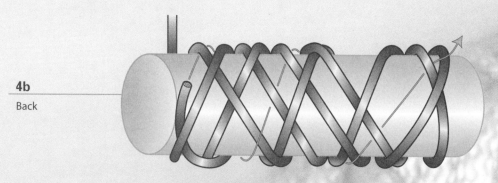

4b

Back

HISTORY

Graumont and Hensel wrote
that they were tying such
elaborate THs as this aboard sailing
ships at the beginning of the twentieth
century, and it is likely that they were in
fact rediscovering knots done long before
that time. This method, however, was
published by Chas. L. Spencer (1946
reprint of his 1934 book, **Knots, Splices
& Fancy Work**) from a description
sent to him by Captain E.W.
Denison, RN.

0

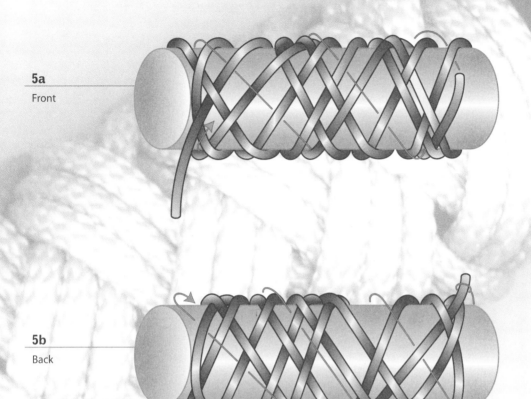

5a

Front

5b

Back

6

<105>

UNIVERSAL TURK'S HEAD CHART

APPLICATIONS

It is useful to have memorized a few handy Turk's head starts, so that you can tie them directly in the hand whenever they are needed. There is no need, however, to master every possible large Turk's head or to pin them out over flat diagrams (with all that unwanted surplus cord), when you might use this universal Turk's head knot chart.

HISTORY

This versatile knot chart was devised by Frank Harris[IGKT] of Charlton in South East London, England, who published it in Issue No. 12 of *Knotting Matters* (July 1985).

METHOD

1 Copy the chart (fig. 1) onto firm paper or flexible card which can be used repeatedly, scaling it up or down to have as many leads and bights as you imagine you will ever need.

2 Wrap it around the foundation for your planned Turk's head (fig. 2) and note carefully where the paper's leading edge meets the numbered bights: in the illustration it coincides with 11, so this knot will have 11 bights.

3 Now wrap and pin your cord around the knot pattern to include as many leads as will suit your purpose, turning back when the furthest corner of any numbered lead square is reached (for example, 9 bights, as illustrated). Keep in mind the Law of the Common Divisor (see p. 83), and also comply with the O-U-O sequence marked on your chart, unless you are prepared to use more than a single strand (in which case be informed by the Rule of the Greatest Common Factor, see p. 83).

PRACTICAL HINT: Draw your squares on the chart to a definite scale, say 1cm (or ½in) and, after making just one knot cycle around the foundation, you will be able to work out how much cord is required to complete the knot. You can use any combination of plain or coloured cords, doubled or tripled. This chart can even be used to create herringbone or twill (O-O-U-U-O-O) weaves.

<106>

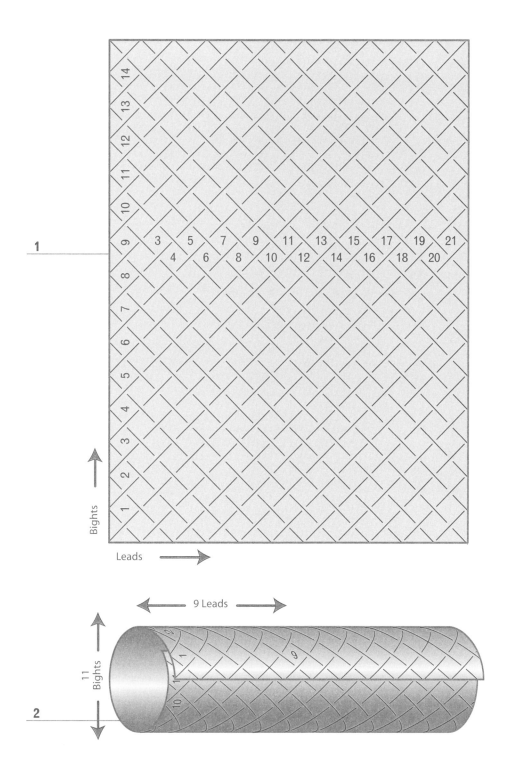

Bights

Leads

9 Leads

11 Bights

<107>

MATS AND HITCHING

MATS

Knotted mats, tied in material that irons flat, are used as tableware coasters. In coarser material, they can serve as doormats. They will also prevent wear and tear, wherever that is desirable, and have even taken the place of oven gloves or a trivet to handle and support hot pans or dishes. Then again, they may be stuck or sewn as embellishments onto uniforms or fancy dress, or tied in interesting materials and framed to make attractive wall decorations.

Mats have been knotted for longer than anyone can recall. Although truly ancient specimens may no longer exist – due to the perishable nature of the materials in which they were tied – IGKT co-founder Des Pawson has begun to collect those he comes across; and he has found similarities between an English one from Appledore in Devonshire and another seen in New Bedford, USA.

Round mat

HITCHING

Spanish and ring hitching usefully covers uninteresting or unsightly rails, rings or other similar objects to render them attractive, hard-wearing and slip-resistant. Needle hitching may be compact, looking a lot like knitting; but it can also be executed with an open pattern to reveal the object within (such as a vulnerable bottle, jar or jug), providing protection against knocks, and some ornamentation, but preserving the appearance of whatever is enclosed. It does not even have to be done with a needle; rope fenders for boats are customarily hitched by hand over a core of junk strands seized roughly to the required shape.

Spanish hitching variation with clove hitches

CARRICK MAT

METHOD

This can easily be tied in the hand as shown (figs. 1–2), resulting in the knot known as a full carrick bend (see *The Hamlyn Book of Knots*). Follow the initial lead around with the working end alongside the standing end (fig. 3) for a two, three or more ply version. This may also be regarded as a flattened 3L x 4B Turk's head; indeed, it is another way to tie that knot.

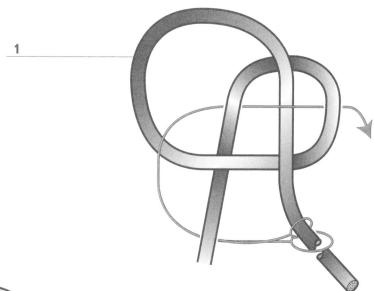

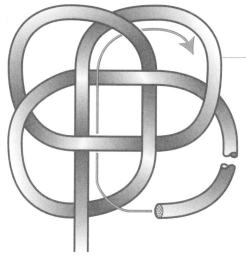

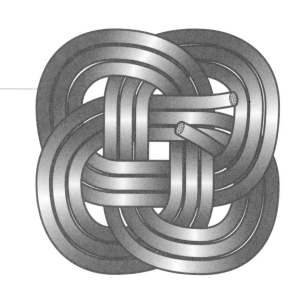

<111>

ROUND MAT

METHOD

This too can be tied directly in the hand. Care with the
O-U-O sequence (figs. 1–3) results in a flattened 3L x 5B
Turk's head, which can also be tied this way.

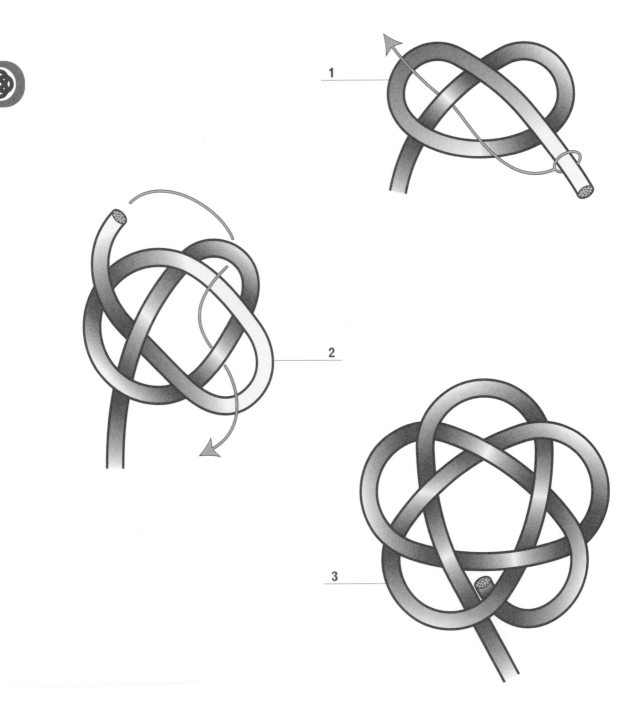

<112>

OCEAN PLAIT MAT

METHOD

Lay the cord on a flat surface and follow the layout and tucks shown (figs. 1–3). No diagram or pins are necessary.

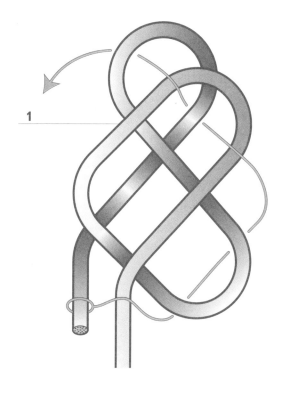

1

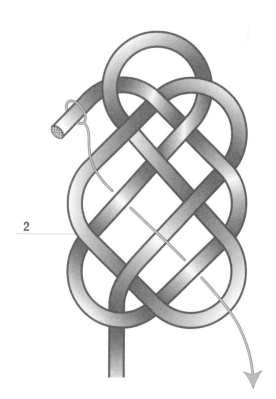

2

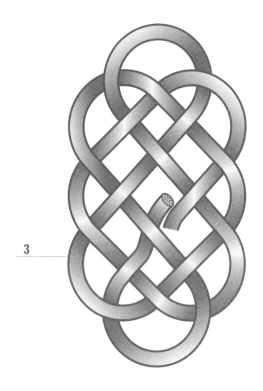

3

<113>

OVAL MAT

METHOD

Lay the cord on a flat surface, taking care to reproduce exactly the interwoven three loop layout (figs. 1–2), and tuck as shown (fig. 3). If done correctly, the final tuck (fig. 4) should be a locking tuck which goes O-U-O-U-O-U-O via a regular ladder of knot parts. Follow around for a two-ply or more finished product (figs. 5– 6). Tighten to remove all daylight from between the crossing points, when the oval shape will appear.

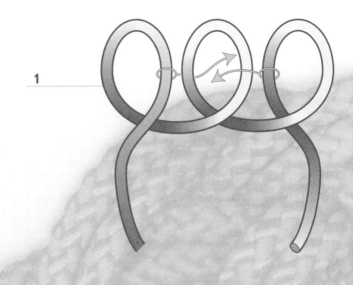

1

2

3

<114>

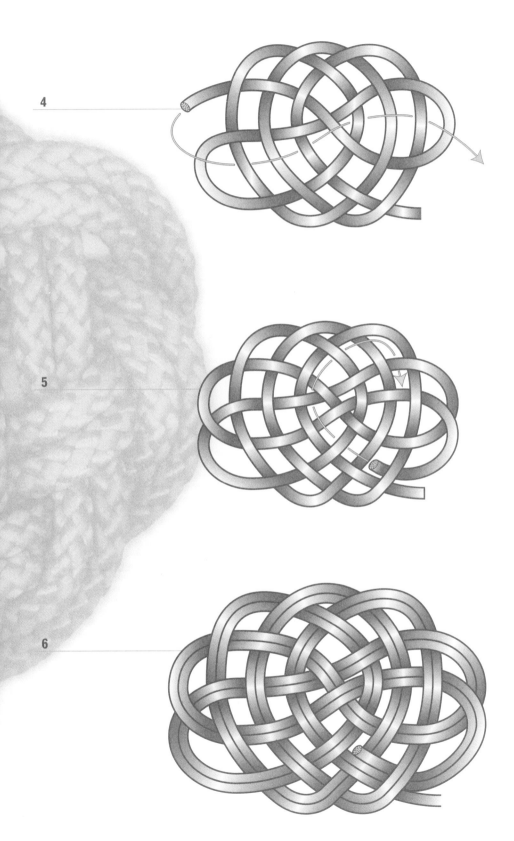

4

5

6

<115>

LONG MAT

METHOD

There is no need for a diagram and pins, but use a flat surface and do not allow loops and bights to become disarranged. Tuck as shown (figs. 1–4) and then insert the locking tuck O-U-O-U-O (fig. 5). Repeat stages 1–4 to extend the knot as far as cord and patience permit. Follow around (fig. 6) to build up the body of the mat, and tighten to eliminate spaces between the knot parts.

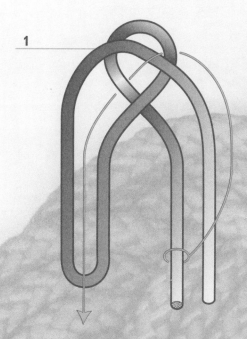

1

HISTORY

This long mat is traditionally called a prolong knot (because its length may be extended). That name seems to have been used first by John Boyd in 1857.

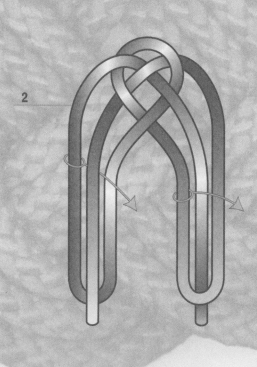

2

<116>

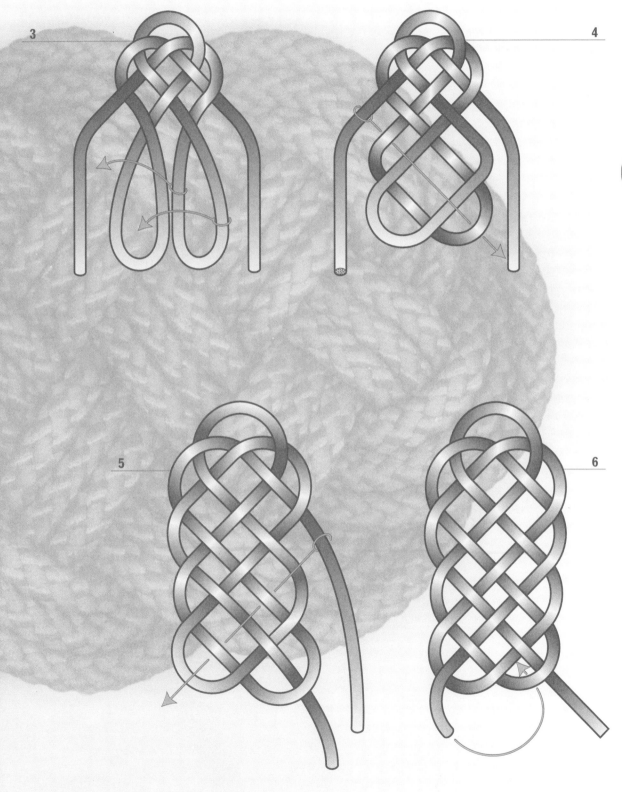

3

4

5

6

<117>

VARIABLE RECTANGULAR MAT PATTERN

METHOD

Copy this pattern, or make up one with different dimensions, using a ruler to ensure straight edges and equidistant T-pins or mapping pins as turning markers for each and every rim and corner bight. Note the V-shape emanating from each corner of this design; it is the key characteristic to this remarkable mat map. Depending upon the proportions, one or more cords may be needed to complete your mat and the Rule of the Greatest Common Factor (see p. 83) seems to apply. Certainly, when I tested a 16 bight x 10 bight (greatest common factor 2), it required two strands; a 12B x 9B (largest common factor 3) needed three strands; and a 20B x 8B (largest common factor 4) took four strands. But, of course, the 19B x 13B specimen illustrated consists of two prime numbers, each only divisible by itself and one (so the greatest common factor is one, and it can therefore be completed with a single strand).

HISTORY

This superb mat pattern was published by Graumont and Wenstrom in 1949, having been submitted to them by Captain G. T. Mundorff, Jnr. of the United States Navy.

<118>

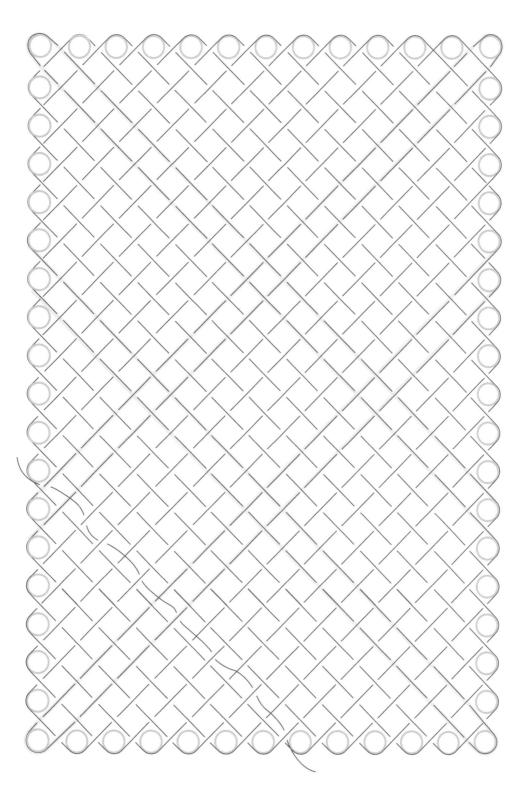

<119>

SPANISH HITCHING

METHOD

A filler strand is wrapped around the foundation and numerous working strands are hitched onto it. Seize sufficient strands to the foundation to cover it when the knotting has been done. There will usually be more than one hand alone can control – but there is a trick to it. Tie the filler strand to a table leg, doorknob or other secure anchorage, up to 2m (2yd) away from the work in hand. Keep it taut with the hand holding the knotting. Use your free hand to flick, tuck and pull each strand in turn snug and tight. Rotate the work, pinning the newly tucked strand in place, and bring the next one around ready to tie off. Periodically – before it reels you in – loosen and lengthen the filler strand on its mooring.

Overhand hitches (fig. 1) look even better with one or more coloured strands included. They spiral around the finished article. Pattern and texture may also be varied by the size and sort of filler strand used (which does not have to be the same as the working ends). Reverse half-hitching (fig. 2) makes a more knobbly surface texture and reveals the spiralling filler strand. Clove hitching (fig. 3) is chunkier still.

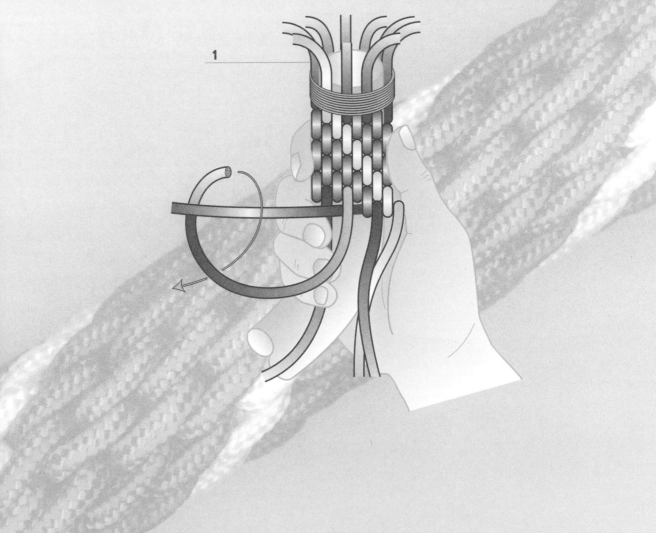

1

HISTORY

Spanish hitching is the name used by Charles L. Spencer as early as 1934. Writers before that seem to have assumed the process was part and parcel of the process of pointing-and-grafting the ends of cables, done aboard ships both to prevent the giant ropes from fraying and to enable them to be passed more easily through hawse pipes aboard ship.

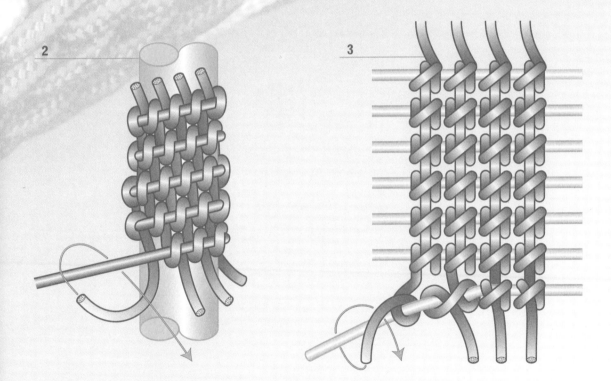

<121>

RING HITCHING

METHOD

So as to negotiate the curve of a ring, hitching must be done in such a way that the encircling cord parts radiate to the outer circumference. The perimeter knotting used to achieve this forms an ornamental outer spine.

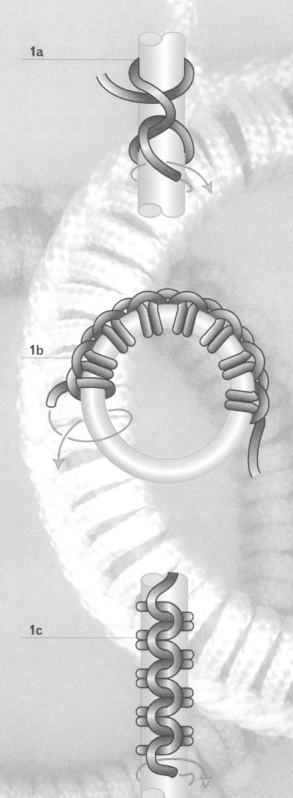

1a

1b

1c

- Alternate hitching (fig. 1a) results in a readily recognized pattern of paired knot parts, from alternate left- and right-hand hitches (figs. 1b–1c).

- Continuous hitching in the same direction (fig. 2) spaces individual knot parts evenly and they emerge from a slimmer spine (figs. 2b–2c) which tends to spiral but is prevented from doing so by the tension applied as it is tied.

- If the ring is thick – or the cord thin – double hitching (figs. 3a–3b) achieves a better effect.

- A series of underhand loops, with the working end threaded through them (figs. 4a–4c) will result in a sort of chain stitch.

- True ringbolt hitching (figs. 5a–5c) incorporates a crest that resembles a three-strand plait, yet it is created with a single cord.

<122>

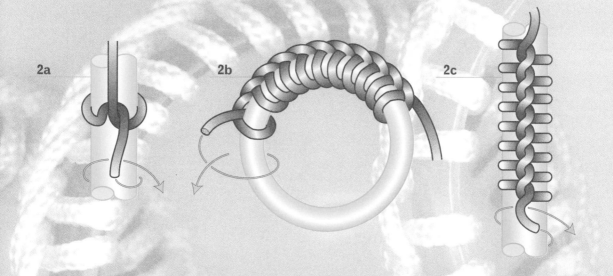

2a

2b

2c

3a

3b

HISTORY

Ring hitching, when used to cover the rings bolted to a ship's deck, was called ringbolt hitching; and the commonest form of alternate left and right hitches was known as kackling (or keckling). The old needlework term for this sort of decorative work was cockscombing.

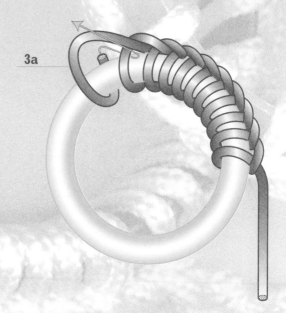

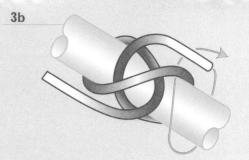

<123>

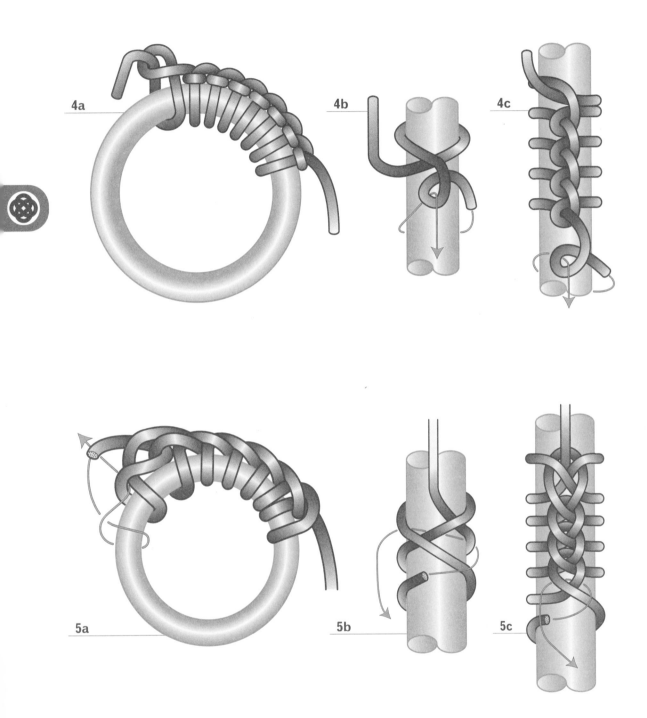

4a

4b

4c

5a

5b

5c

<124>

NEEDLE HITCHING

APPLICATIONS

All needle hitching can be done over a mould –
anything from a thimble to a waste-paper bin.
The mould is then removed to leave a hollow
receptacle. This, depending upon its size and the
material in which it is executed, may then become
anything from a jewellery box to a children's toy
tidy basket.

METHOD

Take a couple of turns around the
object to be covered and then
insert an evenly spaced series of
hitches (fig. 1). The closer these
hitches are to start with, the more
cord (and work) will be entailed,
and the more close-knit will be the
finished texture. Add a second row
of hitches, attached to the first row
as shown (fig. 2), and then
continue around, repeating this
process. Hold each preceding hitch
taut by pressing a thumb upon it,
until the next hitch is in place to
keep it firm. If each newly-formed
hitch is slid up close to one of
those above it, a distinct diagonal
helix will appear in the completed
work. To cope with a core that
increases in diameter, add an extra
hitch at regular intervals. Similarly,
to fit a shrinking core, omit a hitch
now and then. It is generally best
to begin at the widest point.

1

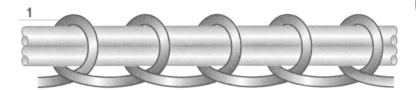

2

<125>

3

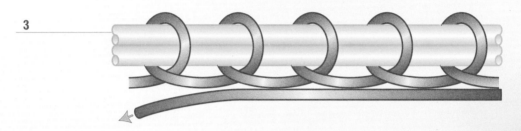

4

Add more substance to basic needle hitching by taking an extra turn around the core before adding each succeeding row of hitches (figs. 3-4). When working down, say, from the neck to the body of a glass bottle – perhaps to make a table lamp – it looks best if the neck is first covered with simple hitching and then this variation is worked over the shoulders of the bottle.

For a more rigid form, hitch in vertical stitched rows (fig. 5). These can be as close as possible (although, in this case, a curved needle may be required).

Conversely, try a mesh-like open pattern. This requires a separate foundation cord or grommet to start and a long tail of a stend (fig. 6). Then, at the commencement of each successive circuit, a winding turn (fig. 7a) is first taken through all of the newly-made meshes before the stend is incorporated – as shown – into the first of the next row of meshes (fig. 7b).

<126>

5

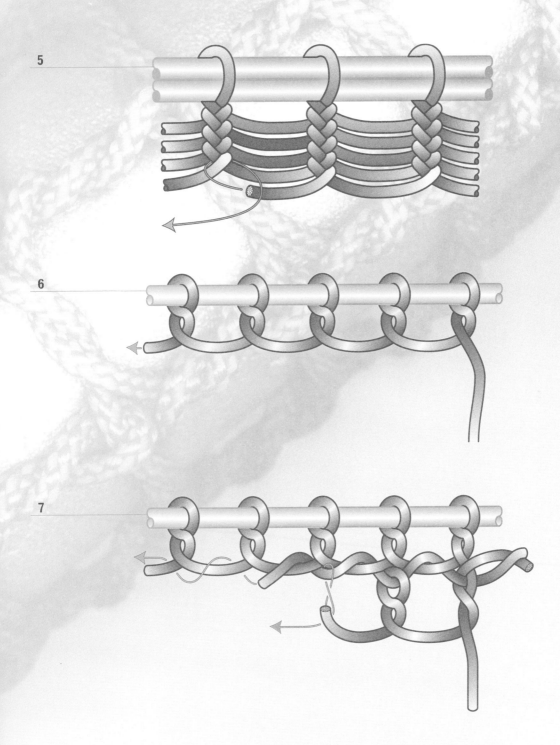

6

7

<127>

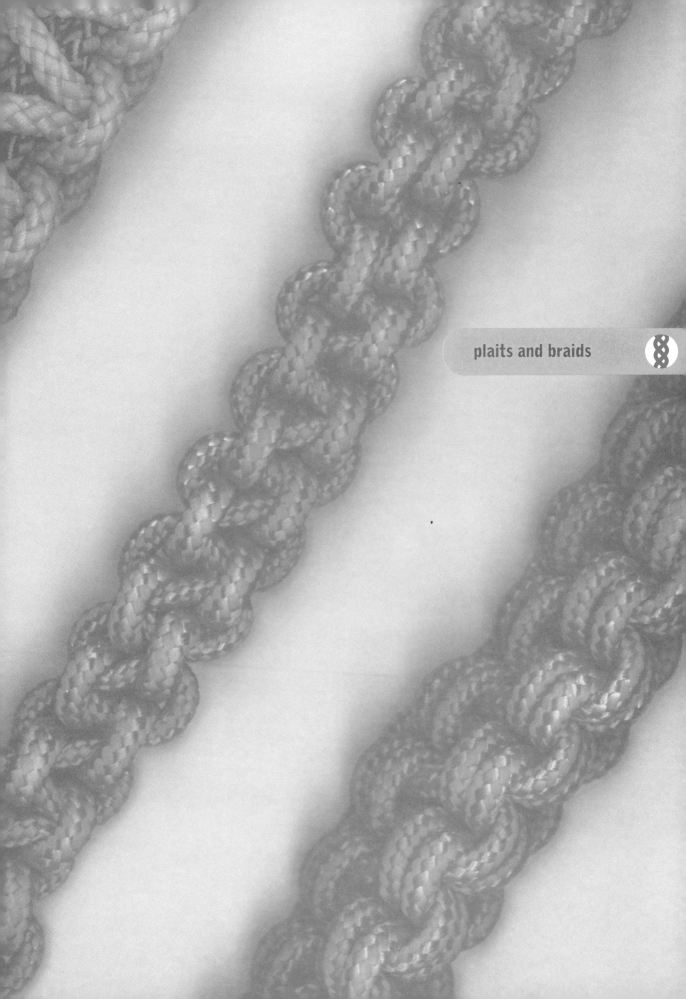

plaits and braids

PLAITS AND BRAIDS

The terms 'plait' and 'braid' mean practically the same nowadays, but there was a time when a plait, plat or pleat (also pronounced 'plat' by sailors) included a fold in cloth, while the label 'braid' was limited to flat plaits. In this book, I too only call something a plait if it is solid, otherwise I refer to it as a braid.

Plaits and braids of various kinds can be applied to window blinds, overhead cisterns and lights as pendant pulls. Depending upon the material used, they may serve as waist ties on dressing gowns or evening gowns, dog leads, horse and cow halters, or curtain tie-backs. With the ends brought around and joined together, they form Turk's head-like rings, which may be slid onto other ropes, or rails, and stitched or glued into position as alternatives to lanyard knots; worn as bracelets or headbands; or made into strong and smart improvized bag handles. Mats, too, may be stitched from long lengths of plaiting or braiding.

Captain John Smith (1626) called plaits 'sinnets'. So did Manwayring (1644), Blanckley (1750), and Dana (1841), with Ashley following suit (1944). Falconer (1769) insisted upon the alternative spelling 'sennit'. And both of these maritime terms are still in use today.

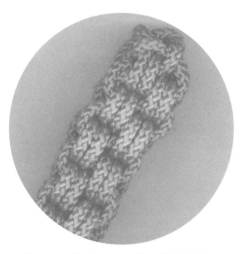

Four-part (eight-strand doubled) plait

Single strand eight-plait trefoil

<130>

SIMPLE CHAIN

METHOD

Start with a slip knot and make a series of draw-loops, each one through the one before (figs. 1-3), taking care to keep the working end on the same side of every draw-loop formed. Young children quickly master this process but may find more enjoyment in then pulling the working end to see the plait unravel once more. To retain the finished plait, tuck the working end through the final draw-loop (fig. 4).

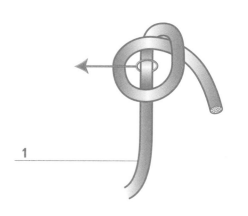

1

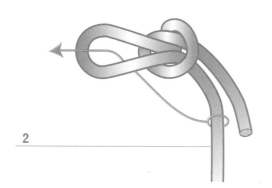

2

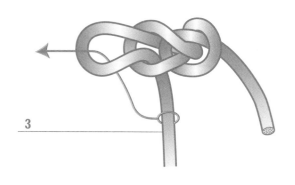

3

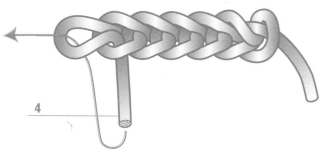

4

<131>

LINKING THE ENDS OF A SIMPLE CHAIN

METHOD

The two ends of a simple chain may be linked, to form a ring or bracelet. Make the tucks shown (figs. 1–2) and finally withdraw the standing end (fig. 3) to lie alongside the working end (fig. 4). Stitch or glue them together, wherever the join will show least.

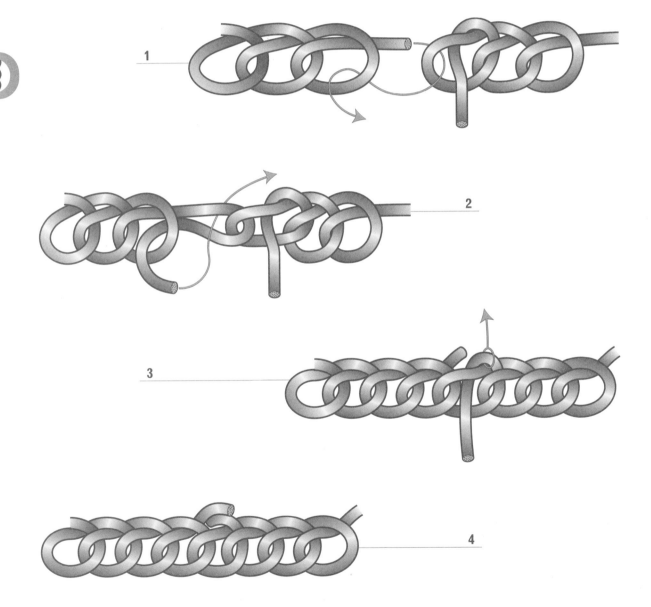

<132>

SINGLE-STRAND STAR KNOT

METHOD

The method previously described of joining the ends of a simple chain (see p. 132) is modified (fig 1), bringing the working end into position to follow around the original lead and double it. Each time an abrupt change of direction occurs (at the nodal rim parts), ensure the working end remains on the same side of the initial lead throughout. The result is a star knot, of any number of rim parts, plaited from a single cord.

1

2

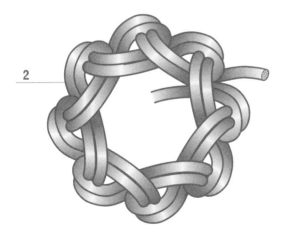

HISTORY

Tom Solly[IGKT] of South Shields in Tyne-&-Wear, England, discovered how to make a star knot from a simple chain plait, publishing the method in the April 1985 issue of *Knotting Matters*. His breakthrough was based upon earlier exploratory work done by George Russell Shaw (1924), Clifford Ashley (1944), Captain Paul Harrison (1965) and S. Clavery (1984).

<133>

DOUBLE CHAIN

METHOD

Start as shown (fig. 1) and pull each new draw-loop through two preceding loops or bights (figs. 2–4). This more solid version (figs. 5–6) looks better all round.

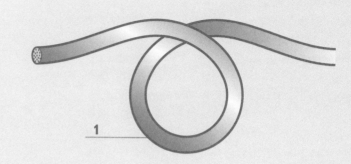

1

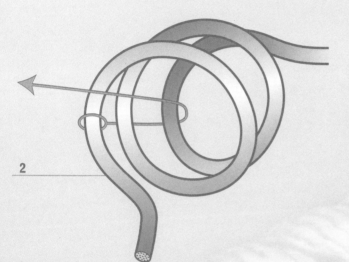

2

HISTORY

A doubled chain plait is still commonly referred to as a doubled trumpet or bugle cord, from its use on bandsmen's uniforms.

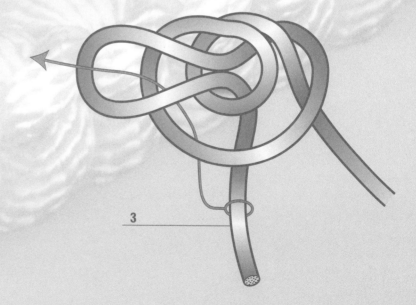

3

<134>

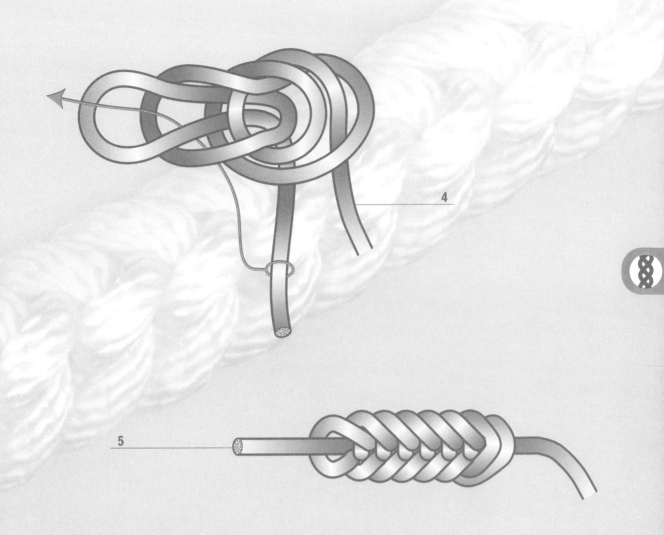

4

5

6

<135>

LINKING THE ENDS OF A DOUBLE CHAIN

METHOD

Make the tucks shown (figs. 1–5), until working end and standing end lie alongside one another (fig. 6) and may be stitched or glued where the join will show least.

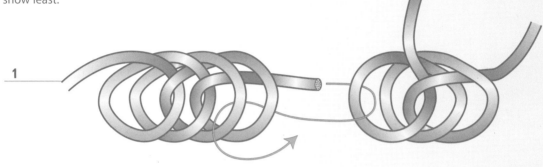

1

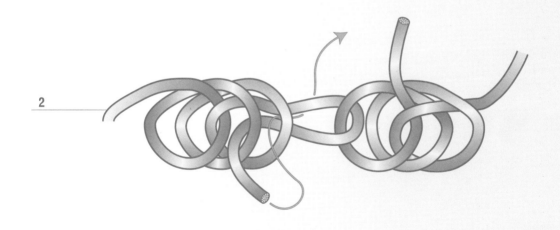

2

3

<136>

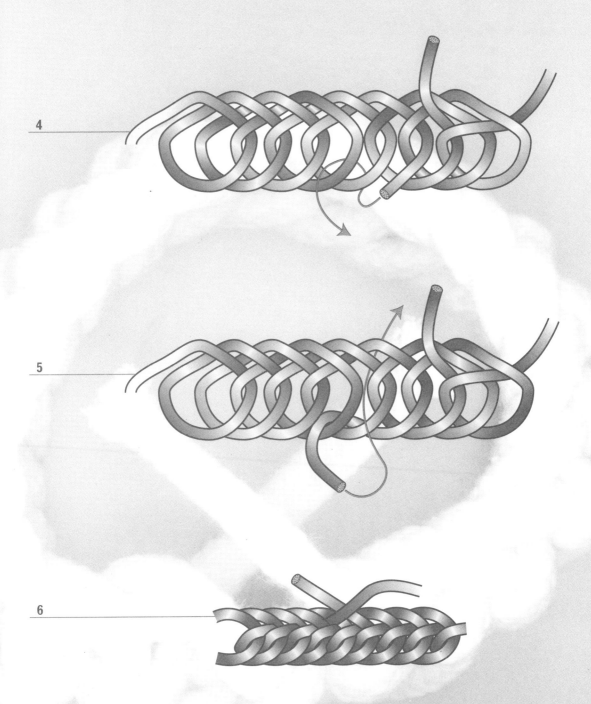

4

5

6

<137>

ZIGZAG BRAID

METHOD

Hitch each strand in turn around the other one (figs. 1–3). At first this appears ugly and unpromising, but as it lengthens the repetitive sawtooth edge turns into a distinctive design (fig. 3). Done in rope it makes a chunky design of bumps and hollows. Executed in fine line, much of the detail goes unobserved but the general outline resembles tatting or crochet.

1
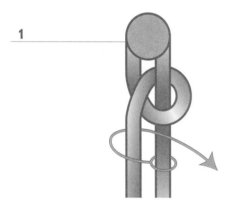

2
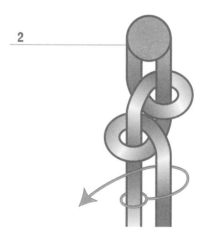

3
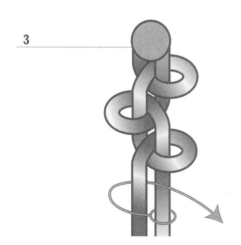

4
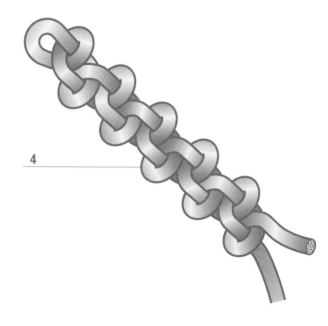

<138>

THREE-STRAND BRAID

METHOD

Arrange the strands as shown (fig. 1), noting that two lie parallel and close together on the left-hand side and the third is on its own on the right-hand side. Bring the *outside* (or upper) left-hand strand down across the front of its partner to lie alongside (but *inside*) the right-hand cord (fig. 2). There are now two right-hand strands and only one left-hand strand. Repeat the process, always moving the upper or outer of the two strands so that it ends up inside the lone strand (figs. 3–5).

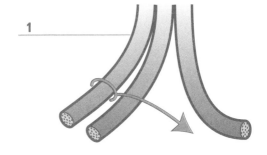

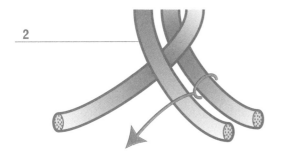

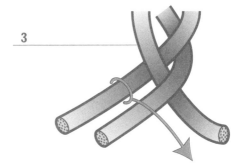

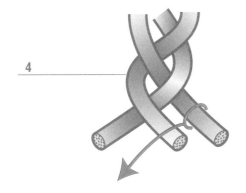

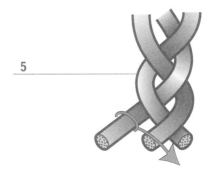

<139>

THREE-STRAND CROWNED PLAIT

METHOD

Tying crown knots (see pp. 28–9) one on top of the other, in the same direction, creates a rope-like plait (fig. 1). Alternate right-hand (clockwise) and left-hand (anti-clockwise) knots produces a plait of roughly triangular cross-section (fig. 2). This shape is more clearcut when it is tied with three pairs of cords (fig. 3). Crown plaiting takes longer to do, and consumes longer lengths of cord, but can also be worked with flat strips of material. Some attractive patterns result when different coloured strands are used.

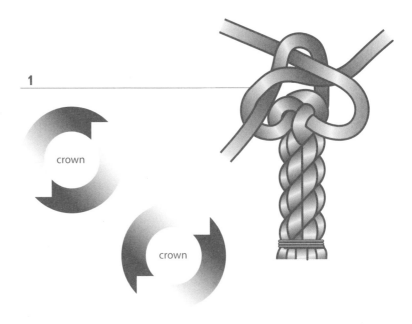

1

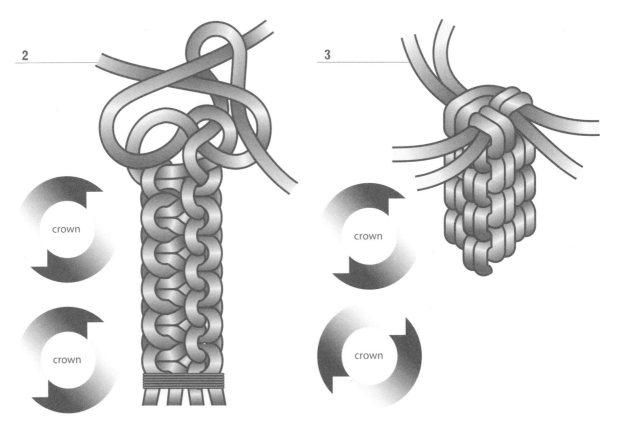

2

3

<140>

FOUR-STRAND BRAID

METHOD

Start as illustrated (fig. 1), arranging the four strands as a LH pair and a RH pair. Bring the LH outer cord *over* to the middle and the RH outer cord *under* to the middle. Cross the centre RH strand *over* the centre LH strand (fig. 2). Repeat the process (fig. 3) as many times as necessary to achieve the desired length of flat braid (fig. 4).

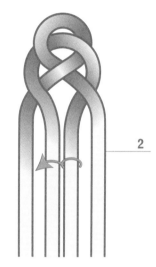

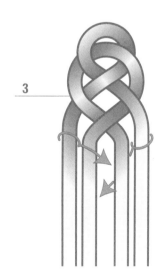

<141>

SOLOMON BAR

METHOD

Attach the four strands to a foundation cord, a ring or other fastening. The two inert middle cords are known as 'filler strands'. Using only the two outer cords as working ends, tie a half knot in the way illustrated (figs. 1–2). Tie a second half knot of opposite handedness (figs. 3–4), ensuring that the working end which crossed from L to R *in front* of the two filler strands returned R to L still to the front. To make the braid without any attachment, middle both strands and hold them together (fig. 5), then tie as before (figs. 6–7)

Repeating this process results in a regular braid with a handsome pattern interlocking front and back (fig. 8). With filler strands of a contrasting colour or material, interesting effects can be made. It is also possible to use strips of wood or plastic that are flat or elliptical in cross-section (e.g. a measuring rule) as fillers, to create, say, a novel picture frame.

To produce a striking spiral (fig. 9), merely make all half knots of the same handedness.

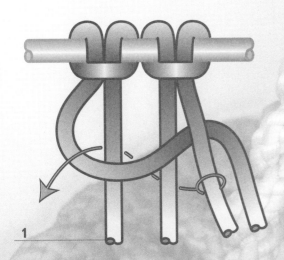

1

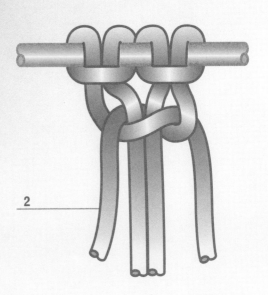

2

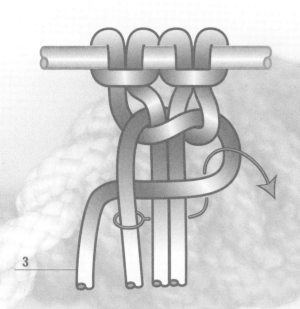

3

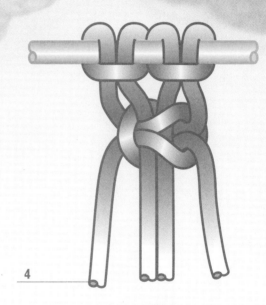

4

HISTORY

The solomon bar is also known
to macramé practitioners as a bannister
bar. Macramé, (say 'Mac-ram-ay') is a
19th-century European word. In the USA it is
more aptly called 'square-knotting', as it
resembles an accumulation of reef knots and the
American name for a reef knot is a square knot.
The craft itself is centuries older, probably
originating with Arab weavers. A painting by
Paul Veronese (1528–88), *The Repast of
Simon the Pharisee* (now in the Louvre)
has in its foreground a cloth with
a deep macramé, border.

<143>

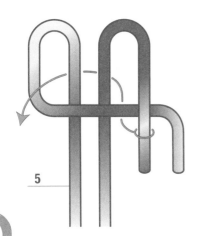

5

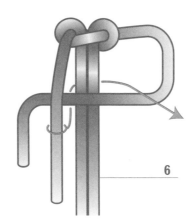

6

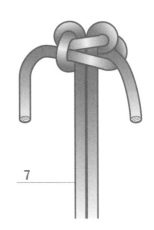

7

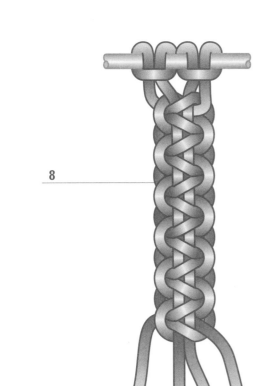

8

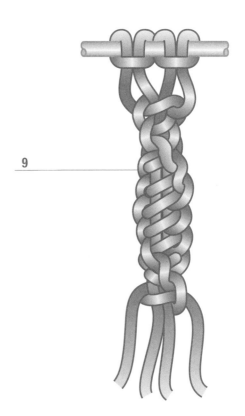

9

<144>

FOUR-STRAND PLAIT

METHOD

Start as shown (fig. 1), with the strands as a left- and right-hand pair. Bring the outer left-hand strand around the back and *up* between the two right-hand strands, returning it to its own side – but now as the *inner* strand (figs. 2–3). Repeat as desired (figs. 3–4) to produce a plait that is generally called 'round', although the cross-section is more nearly square.

1

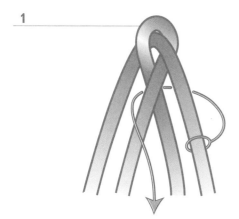

2

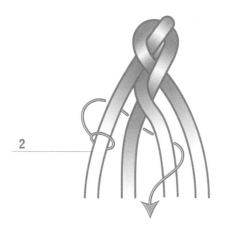

3

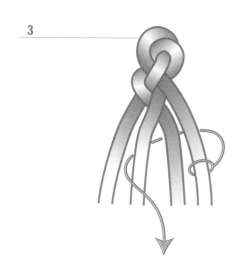

4

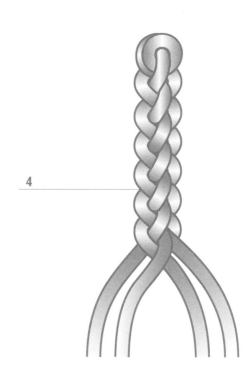

<145>

FOUR-STRAND CROWNED PLAIT

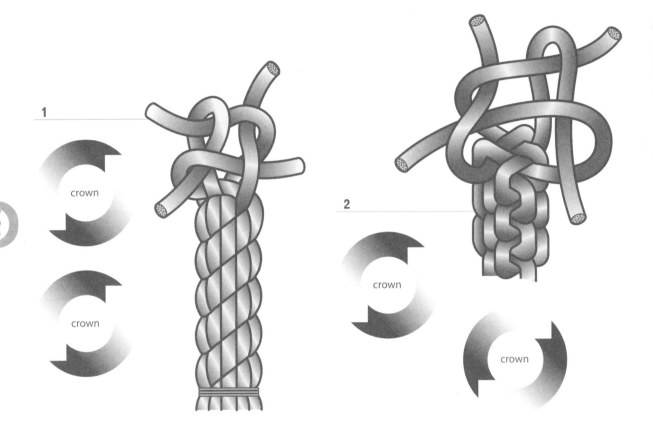

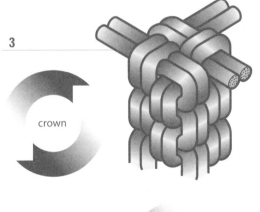

METHOD

Tying four-strand crown knots one after the other, in the same direction, produces a rope-like plait (fig. 1). Alternating the direction of the knots, right-hand (clockwise) and left-hand (anti-clockwise) results in a different surface texture (fig. 2). Doing it with four pairs of strands makes a plait that is distinctly square in cross-section (fig. 3).

<146>

SIX-STRAND PLAIT

METHOD

This is a different way of working from that of previous plaits and braids. Seize six strands, keeping three working ends upright and bending each one of the other three down around an adjacent upright strand (figs. 1a–1b). Note how the downward pointing strands are snugly embedded (like a crown knot minus its locking tuck). Whatever the handedness of this crowning – left-hand (anti-clockwise) in the illustration – bend the three upright strands down the opposite way, at the same time lifting up the first three working ends (figs. 2–4) to trap and hold the second layer of crowning. It requires a little practise to acquire a feel for this awkward sequence of movements, and it is essential to keep track of which three working ends are which (I dab a spot of colour on one trio with a felt-tipped pen), but it is worth the effort to make this solid and good-looking plait (fig. 5).

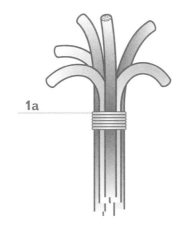

1a

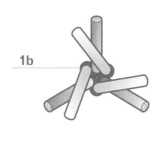

1b

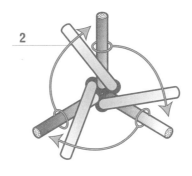

2

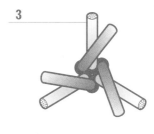

3

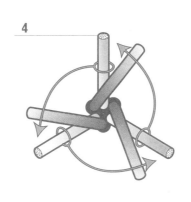

4

5

<147>

EIGHT-STRAND PLAIT

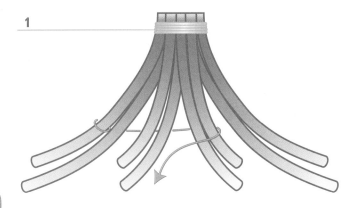

1

METHOD

This is akin to the basic four-strand plait. Seize eight cords and separate them into two batches of four (fig. 1). Starting with the outer (and upper) left-hand strand, take it around the back and then bring it up between the two pairs of right-hand strands, returning it to its own side (but now as the middle left-hand cord). Repeat this with the upper and outer right-hand strand (fig. 2). Continue working with alternate left- and right-hand strands, always taking the upper strand (fig. 3). Pay particular attention to pulling the strand taut where it passes around the back of the work, to produce a splendidly strong and flexible plaited rope of square cross-section (fig. 4).

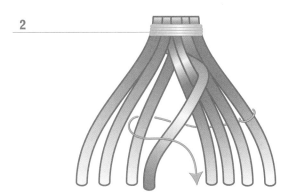

2

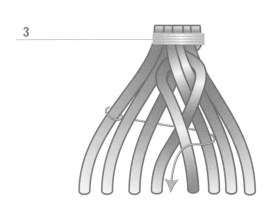

3

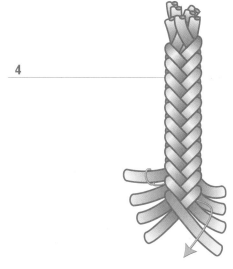

4

<148>

TWO-STRAND, EIGHT-PLAIT GROMMET

METHOD

Tie a simple overhand or thumb knot in a single strand (fig. 1) and continue to tuck the working end repeatedly in the same direction to make a twined ring (figs. 2–3). Now take the working end around a third time, carefully following the groove between the initial two leads. The result is an endless three-strand rope, tied with a single strand, known as a 'Grommet' (fig. 4). Go around once more, increasing the grommet to four strands (fig. 5). Keep it fairly loose, another strand is to be woven into it; even so, the fourth lot of turns will not bed down neatly – but this is not crucial to the finished work.

Take a second strand, which– certainly the first few times this construction is attempted – it is helpful to have in a different colour, and tuck it under two strands, in the opposite direction to the original helix (fig. 5). Continue going around U-U-O-O-U-U (fig. 6) until this second working end is back beside itself at the start. Go around again (fig. 7), creating a second layer of contrary interlacing, alongside and staggered (the width of one strand) from the first circuit (fig. 8). Do a third circuit and a fourth, filling in the gaps (fig. 9). The result ought to be a solid eight-plait grommet (figs. 10a–b) with four ends emerging close together at the start. This is a tricky bit of plaiting. There are so many points where a wrong tuck can be taken – as eyesight misleads, concentration or confidence wavers – that it may not come right at the first or second attempt. I have sailed faultlessly through one in as little as 20 minutes, then, another time, taken two days of frustrating do-and-undo to complete one successfully. Although the eight-plait texture is perfect, it becomes clear using two differently coloured strands that there is a subtle twist in it. This is hardly a flaw; indeed, replace the coloured strand with one that matches the original lead, and it will disappear from sight.

Bury two strands and knot the remaining two together. The result makes an unusual lanyard ornament to use as a necklace.

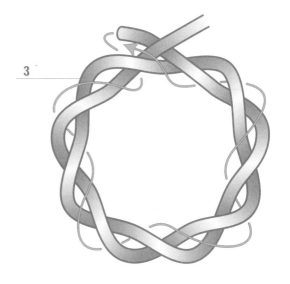

<149>

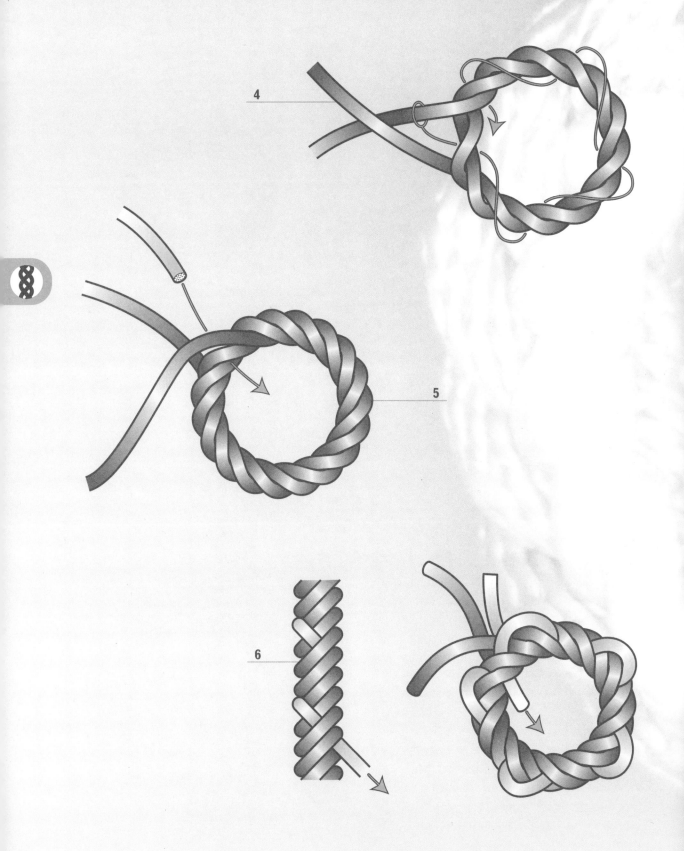

<150>

7

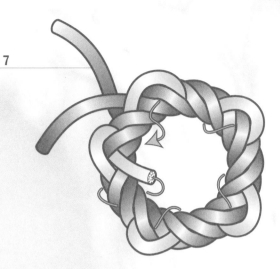

HISTORY

Using actual three-strand hawser-laid rope the earliest grommets (sailors said 'grummits') were used aboard ship as mast hoops, block straps, and to reinforce eyes in canvas sails. In this century, however, they were demoted to being used by the passengers on luxury ocean liners to play deck quoits. The plaited one shown here was suggested by Clifford Ashley as a Turk's head variation.

8

<151>

9

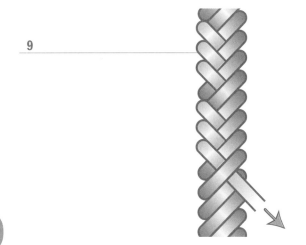

10a

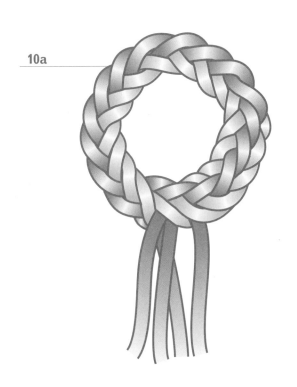

10b

<152>

SINGLE-STRAND, EIGHT-PLAIT TREFOIL

METHOD

First understand the preceding two-strand, eight-plait grommet. The only extra contrivance is the seemingly impossible overhand or thumb knot incorporated here. Simply tie the knot (fig. 1) before wrapping and tucking to arrive at a four-ply grommet (fig. 2). Then, overlap and tuck both ends back under TWO strands, so that their elbows interlock (fig. 2 a). Complete two U-U-O-O-U-U circuits in one direction with one working end, and two the other way with the other working end. Bring them out close together, add a two-strand single wall knot and tie the ends together with a doubled fisherman's knot (fig. 5).

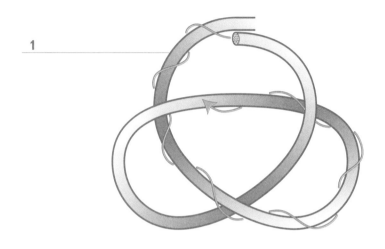

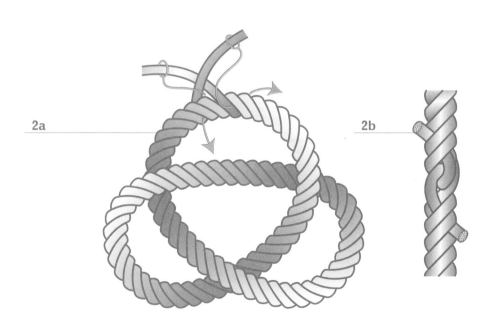

<153>

3

HISTORY

This remarkable creation is
only a few years old. I first spotted
one – tied in rope – at the IGKT's 14th
Annual General Meeting, held in May 1996
at Scouting's international campsite, Gilwell
Park, in Essex, England. It had been made by
Jeff Wyatt. He and Charlie Smith, between
them, generously showed me the trick of it;
and, not realizing that it was actually tied
with two strands, I went home and
produced my single-strand
version.

<154>

GLOSSARY

Bellrope	In knot tying, this is the sort of plaited and knotted lanyard attached to the clapper of a boat or ship's bell (but not a church bellrope).
Bight	Strictly a U-shaped bend in rope or smaller cordage; also refers to the scallop-shaped rim parts of a Turk's head.
Braid	Strands interwoven with one another to form an essentially flat strip (see also **Plait**).
Button knot	A small stopper knot which, being bulbous, might serve as a button (see also **Globe knot**).
Capsize (of knots)	To become deformed due to incorrect tying or tightening.
Cord	Line under 25mm (1in) circumference or approximately 10mm (½in) diameter (see also **Small stuff**).
Cordage	A general term for all kinds of cord, line or rope.
Core	The filler in the centre of some rope and cordage, made from fibres or monofilaments.
Crowning	A knotting process which turns the strands of a rope or plait back upon themselves.
Doubling	Following the initial lead around once more with the working end.
Fray	Deliberately or accidentally to allow a rope or cord to unlay, so that its component strands and yarns are separated.
Globe knot	Large bulbous knot which acts as a spherical covering (see also **Button knot**).
Grommet	A rope ring.
Heart	See **Core**.
Knot	The general name for what results when any rope and cord is deliberately tied; although strictly speaking the word does not include two joined ropes (which are 'bent' together) or mooring ropes and similar attachments (which are 'hitched').
Lanyard	Short length of cord used to lash, secure or suspend an item of equipment or ornamentation.
Lead	The direction, including any over-under-over-under (O-U-O-U) tucking sequence, taken by cordage around or through an object or knot; hence 'to follow a lead' is generally to double (treble, quadruple, etc.) an existing knot.
Line	A general term for any rope or cord with a specific function (e.g. washing *line*, tow *line*, mooring *line*).
Matthew Walker	The name of an 18th-century individual – identity now lost – who, in knotlore, seems to have been the first man to have had a knot named after him.
Middle	To fold a rope or cord in half prior to use, and so locate the centre.
Part	Any inactive section of a knot; also synonymous with the word 'lead' when used to indicate the width or length of a Turk's head.
Plait	Strands interwoven with one another to form a solid cross-section (see also **Braid**).
Rope	Cordage over 25mm (1in) in circumference or about 10mm (½in) in diameter and thicker than cord.
Small stuff	A casual imprecise term used by knot tyers for any cordage not large enough to be defined as rope.
Standing end	The inactive end of a cord or rope, opposite to the working end.
Stopper knot	A knot tied in the end of a rope or plait to prevent it fraying or pulling out of any attachment.
String	Domestic quality small cord or twine.
Trebling	Following the initial lead of a knot twice more.
Turk's head	The generic name for the largest family of knots; so called because the basic ones were once thought to resemble turbans.
Walling	A knotting process which raises a reinforcing ridge around the rope or plait in which it is tied.
Working end	Active end of a cord or rope, directly involved in twisting, interweaving or tucking a braid, plait or knot.

<155>

BIBLIOGRAPHY

Although there are older written references to many individual fancy knots, books about decorative knotwork are a 20th-century phenomenon. This is odd because it is hardly new: Leonardo da Vinci drew ornate knot patterns, medieval weavers finished their carpets with knotted fringes, 18th- and 19th-century sailors practised marlinespike seamanship; but, if contemporary writers and artists knew about such skilful handicraft, they seem not to have been commissioned to sketch and describe it. Still, a number of comparatively modern publications are obtainable in bookshops, the older ones reprinted (sometimes revised, in new covers) and where necessary translated. The contents of this book have been influenced by the following writers, living and dead, whose original publications I gratefully acknowledge.

PRIMARY SOURCES

Ashley, Clifford W., *The Ashley Book of Knots*, Doubleday, Doran & Co. Inc. (1944)/Faber & Faber (1947)

Bigon, Mario, and Regazzoni, Guido, *The Century Guide to Knots*, Century Publishing Co. Ltd. (1982)

Chen, Lydia, *Chinese Knotting*, Echo Publishing Co. Ltd. (1982)

Field[IGKT], Brian, *Breast Plate Designs*, IGKT (1985)

Franklin[IGKT], Eric, *Turksheads the Traditional Way*, IGKT (1985)

Graumont, Raoul, and Wenstrom, Elmer, *Square Knot Handicraft Guide*, Cornell Maritime Press (1949)

International Guild of Knot Tyers, *Knotting Matters* (quarterly journal/October 1982 to date)

Lever, Darcy, *The Young Sea Officer's Sheet Anchor*, London (1808)

Short, Eirian, *Introducing Macramé*, B.T. Batsford (1970)

Spencer, Chas. L. *Knots, Splices & Fancy Work*, Brown, Son & Ferguson (1934)

Warner[IGKT], Charles, *A Fresh Approach to Knotting and Ropework*, published by the author (1992)

SECONDARY SOURCES (REFERRED TO IN THE ABOVE PUBLICATIONS)

Blanckley, Thomas Riley, *A Naval Expositor*, London (1750)

Boyd, John McNeill, *Manual for Naval Cadets*, London (1857)

Brady, Wm. N. (Boatswain, U.S. Navy), *The Naval Apprentice's Kedge Anchor*, New York (1841)

Dana, R. H., *Seaman's Friend*, New York (1841)

Falconer, William, *An Universal Dictionary of the Marine*, London (1769)

Little, E. N., *Log Book Notes* (1889)

Manwayring, Sir Henry, *The Sea-man's Dictionary*, London (1644)

Norie, J. W., *Mariner's New and Complete Naval Dictionary* (1804)

Smith, Captaine John, *An Accidence for Young Sea-men*, London (1626)

Todd & Whall, *Practical Seamanship for the Merchant Marine*, London (1896)

Wetjen, Albert R., *Fiddlers' Green*, (1941)

FURTHER RECOMMENDED READING

Aldridge[IGKT], George, *Making Solid Sennits*, self-published c.1990 (undated)

Budworth[IGKT], Geoffrey, *The Hamlyn Book of Knots*, Reed International Books Ltd. (1997)

Carey, Jacqui, *Creative Kumihimo*, Carey Company (1994)

Edwards[IGKT], Ron, *Knots - Useful and Ornamental*, The Rams Skull Press, Australia (1993)

Findley[IGKT], Gladys, & Blandford[IGKT], Percy, *Macramé, Projects,* Dryad Press (1986)

Follet, Véronique, *Friendship Bracelets*, Search Press Ltd. (1995)

Franklin[IGKT], Eric, *Nylon Novelties*, IGKT (1995)

Grainger[IGKT], Stuart E., *Creative Ropecraft*, G. Bell & Sons Ltd. (1975)

Grainger[IGKT], Stuart E., *Knotcraft*, IGKT (1989)

Grainger[IGKT], Stuart E., *Ropefolk*, IGKT (undated)

Grainger[IGKT], Stuart E., *Turkshead Alternatives*, self-published (1991)

Grainger[IGKT], Stuart E., *Knotted Fabrics*, self-published (1997)

Graumont, Raoul, & Hensel, John, *Encyclopedia of Knots and Fancy Rope Work*, Cornell Maritime Press (1939)

Griend[IGKT], Pieter van de, *S4C (single-strand regular spherical knots)*, self-published (1991)

Griend[IGKT], Pieter van de, *The Wee Light House Knot*, self-published (1993)

Halifax[IGKT], John, *Something Different (Button Knots)*, self-published (1991)

Hall[IGKT], Tom, *Turk's-Head Knot Tips*, self-published (1990)

Harrison, Capt. P.P.O., *The Harrison Book of Knots*, Brown, Son & Ferguson Ltd. (1964)

Hin[IGKT], Floris, *The Colour Book of Knots*, Macmillan (1982)

Hussey-Smith, Gypsy, *Rope & Twine Crafts*, Thomas C. Lothian Pty. Ltd. (1993)

<156>

Jones[IGKT], Colin, *The Fender Book*, published by the author (1996)

Martin, Catherine, *Kumihimo - Japanese Silk Braiding Techniques*, Old Hall Press (1986)

Michigan State University, *Marlinespikes and Monkey's Fists*, The Board of Trustees (1994)

Owen, Peter, *The Book of Decorative Knots*, Lyons & Burford (1994)

Owen, Roderick, *The Big Book of Sling and Rope Braids*, Cassell (1995)

Scott[IGKT], Harold, *On Various Cruciform Turks-Heads*, self-published (1997)

Shaw, George Russell, *Knots - Useful & Ornamental*, Bonanza Books (1924)

Silver, Lynette, *Making Friendship Bands*, Milner Dodgem Books (1994)

Smith, Hervey Garrett, *The Marlinespike Sailor*, The Rudder Publishing Co. (1960)

Welch, Nancy, *Tassels - The Fanciful Embellishment*, Lark Books (1992)

Zosma, Luanne Gaykowski, *Marlinespikes and Monkey's Fists*, Michigan State University Museum (1994)

REAL KNOT THEORY

Separate mention is merited for the many unrivalled publications by A. Georg Schaake and John C. Turner[IGKT] (with additional contributions from Tom Hall[IGKT] and D.A. Sedgwick), jointly published (1988–1991) and obtainable from the Department of Mathematics and Statistics, University of Waikato, Hamilton New Zealand. With rigorous arithmetic and algebra, the authors have developed working algorithms for tying real braids, pineapple knots and Turk's heads, etc. Their 14 manuals are not just fascinating to students of maths; they are the key to complex knots and braids for practical knot tyers.

PAWSON KNOTTING MUSEUM

Anyone seeking further inspiration should contact Des and Liz Pawson[IGKT], trading as Footrope Knots at 501 Wherstead Road, Ipswich, Suffolk IP2 8LL, England (Tel: 01473 690 090). Founder members of the IGKT, in addition to supplying tools, materials and advice, they will show you around their unique ropework museum free of charge. They opened it in 1996 stating: "We believe that the world should recognize the art and skill of knots".

THE INTERNATIONAL GUILD OF KNOT TYERS

The Guild was established by 27 individuals in April 1982 and now has a membership approaching 1,000 in countries from Australia to Zimbabwe. It is a UK registered educational charity and anyone interested in knots may join.

Guild members are a friendly crowd, novice and expert alike, brought together by their common pursuit of knot tying. Members within travelling distance may enjoy two major weekend meetings held in England each year, with talks, demonstrations and tuition, where tools, cordage and books (new and second-hand) are also bought and sold or swapped. In areas where many Guild members live, national or regional branches have been formed, and these arrange more frequent gatherings and activity programmes.

The thinly scattered worldwide IGKT members keep in touch via a members' handbook and a quarterly magazine, *Knotting Matters*, which is full of informed articles, expert tips, letters, editorial comment, news and views about everything imaginable on the knot tying scene. The Guild also sells its own instructional publications, postcards and other knotting supplies by mail order.

A few Guild members trade commercially in specialized rope and cordage, tools, and books (new, second-hand and rare) unobtainable elsewhere, also selling ready-made or made-to-order knot display boards and other ropework items. Their expert advice is freely available to customers and Guild members.

For further details and an application form, contact:

Nigel Harding (IGKT Hon. Secretary)

16 Egles Grove

Uckfield

Sussex TN22 2BY

England

Tel: (01825) 760 425

Note that cordage used to tie the knots illustrated in this book was obtained from:

K. J. K. Ropeworks, (Kevin Keatley[IGKT]), Town Living Farmhouse, Puddington, Tiverton,

Devon EX16 8LL, England

Tel: (01864) 860 692 (24-hours)/Fax: (01864) 860 994.

<157>

INDEX

<158>

<159>

END COMMENT

The ingenious eight-plait trefoil described on page 153 is proof that knotting is no dying art or fossilized craft. Knot tyers continue to find superb new knots. After thousands of years practising them, we may know only half of all there is to discover about knotting. For those of us under its spell, it is a magnificent obsession. In 1876 the mathematician Peter Guthrie Tait wrote, "The subject of 'beknottedness' is a very much more difficult and intricate one than at first sight one is inclined to think." If you have enjoyed the contents of this book, then you too are well on the way to becoming…

BESOTTED BY BEKNOTTEDNESS.